Cambridge Topics in Geography

Editors Alan R.H. Baker, Emmanual College, Cambridge
Colin Evans, King's College School, Wimbledon

Environment, Resources and Conservation

Susan Owens
Lecturer in Geography, University of Cambridge
and
Peter L. Owens
Lecturer in Geography, University of Sheffield

D1407385

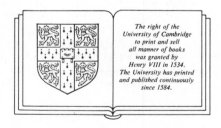

The right of the
University of Cambridge
to print and sell
all manner of books
was granted by
Henry VIII in 1534.
The University has printed
and published continuously
since 1584.

Cambridge University Press
Cambridge
New York   Port Chester   Melbourne   Sydney

Published by the Press Syndicate of the University of Cambridge
The Pitt Building, Trumpington Street, Cambridge CB2 1RP
40 West 20th Street, New York, NY 10011, USA
10 Stamford Road, Oakleigh, Melbourne 3166, Australia

First published 1991

Printed in Great Britain at the University Press, Cambridge

British Library cataloguing-in-publication data
Owens, Susan E. and Owens, Peter L.
Environment, resources and conservation. – (Cambridge topics in geography).
1. Environment
I. Title
333.7

Library of Congress cataloging-in-publication data
Applied for

ISBN 0 521 30912 3 hardback
ISBN 0 521 31378 3 paperback

DS

Acknowledgements
The publishers would like to thank the following for permission to reproduce illustrations:
Frank Lane Picture Agency: W. Broadhurst, p.6, Silvestris Fotoservice, p.44;
Cambridgeshire Wildlife Trust, p.14 (top); Shell Photographic Service, p.15; National
Society for Clean Air (NCSA), p.26; The Swedish Institute (André Maslennikov), p.50;
International Freelance Library (John Smith), p.59; Committee of Aerial Photography,
University of Cambridge, pp. 60, 73 bottom left, bottom right; Julian Tudor Hart, p.63;
British Coal Opencast Executive, p.69; Richard Denyer, pp.74 (bottom), 83 (right);
Peter Wakely, p.76 bottom left, right; National Railway Museum, p.79 (top); British Gas,
p.90 (bottom); cartoonist David Haldane, and the Green Party, 10 Station Parade,
Balham High Road, London SW12 9AZ tel. 081–673 0045, p.91; Greenpeace
Communications Ltd, p.95; National Institute of Public Health and Safety, Netherlands,
p.102.

Other items are reproduced by permission as follows:
pp.44, 48–49: extracts from *Acid Rain – A Review of the Phenomenon in the EEC and
Europe*, Environmental Resources Ltd, published by Graham & Trotman, London, on
behalf of The Commission of the European Communities; Fig.2.1, 'Hierarchy of Needs'
from *Motivation and Personality* by H. Maslow, © 1954 Harper & Row, Publishers, Inc.,
© 1970 Abraham H. Maslow, reprinted by permission of Harper & Row, Publishers, Inc.;
Figs 2.3, 3.3, 7.3, 7.6 reproduced with the permission of the Controller of Her Majesty's
Stationery Office.

Every effort has been made to reach copyright holders; the publishers would be glad to
hear from anyone whose rights they have unknowingly infringed.

The authors would like to thank the staff of the University of Cambridge Department of
Geography Drawing Office for their help in preparing some of the maps and diagrams.

Contents

1 The environmental debate

A revolution in thinking about resources and the environment has occurred during the past quarter of a century. Environmentalism is no longer the preserve of a small minority, variously regarded as 'far-sighted' or 'cranky'; it has become a major public issue, firmly established on the political agenda at national and international level. But after several decades of attention and legislation, many environmental problems remain stubbornly difficult to solve. Sometimes this is due to novelty or complexity but often, as the environmentalist Barbara Ward once pointed out:

> . . . the difficulty is not to identify the remedy, because the remedy is now understood. The problems are rooted in the economy and society.[1]

This book focuses on the social, economic and political complexities of resource use and environmental issues. It is centred on three case studies of resource use and pollution in the developed world, each of which shows how difficult it can be to translate theoretical concepts into practical environmental policies. The material is necessarily selective and issue-oriented. Readers seeking comprehensive analysis of natural resources or environmental issues at a global scale should refer to some of the excellent texts listed under 'Further reading' at the end of this book.

The remainder of this chapter outlines some important developments in the global environmental debate, to set a wider context for the more specific issues that follow. In Chapter 2, important fundamental problems for environmental policy, which recur in all three case studies, are drawn together. Chapter 3 introduces the case studies and provides some theoretical background on pollution, resource depletion and ecosystem management. The case studies – 'acid rain' in Europe, exploitation of Britain's coal reserves, and resource management in the Norfolk Broads – follow in Chapters 4 to 6. Finally, in Chapter 7, progress in dealing with environmental problems, and major policy achievements, are reviewed, and prospects for the future considered.

The beginnings of concern

Modern environmentalism was born in the 1960s. There have been many attempts to explain the sudden upsurge in concern about resource depletion and pollution – themselves not new problems – which took place towards the end of that decade. No single cause can readily be identified, but a combination of physical reality, analytical capability, mass media interest, and a wave of 'public participation' in Western democracies, probably provided the preconditions for political action. Certainly there were new and alarming physical manifestations of environmental decay in the 1960s, and a constantly improving capacity

Pollution from a chemical plant in north-west England.

to identify their long-term implications. Bio-accumulation of pesticides, oil pollution, heavy-metal poisoning and the 'death' of lakes and rivers were all much publicised and contributed to growing unease about irreversible damage to the biosphere, which might ultimately threaten the human race itself. As Francis Sandbach argues in his analysis of environmentalism:

> . . . the importance of the disturbing revelations of the late 1960s was not only that they suddenly uncovered a mass of hitherto unsuspected environmental problems, but also that they created a sense of insecurity; alarmism and predictions of catastrophe inevitably aroused fear.[2]

Unease was intensified by the first evocative images of the Earth from space, emphasising its essentially finite nature and vulnerability. Perhaps most important of all, an affluent, educated and politically active post-war generation was ready to take up 'the environment' as a cause. Whatever the precise combination of factors involved, the effects were dramatic. Media coverage, demand for environmental literature, and pressure group membership soared (Fig. 1.1). The 1972 Stockholm Conference on the Human Environment received unprecedented attention and many governments responded to mounting political pressure by creating 'environmental' departments and enacting major new legislation.

Eco-catastrophe or cornucopia?

Environmentalism in the late 1960s and early 1970s was characterised by doom-laden warnings of imminent ecological disaster and demands for urgent, often drastic, global action to avert this fate. Among the

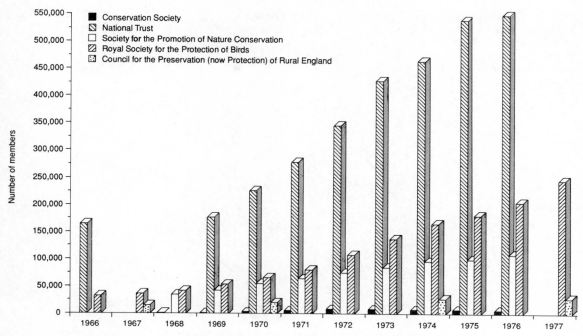

Number of members

Fig. 1.1 Membership of selected environmental groups in the UK, 1966–77.

Source: Based on figures in **Sandbach, F.** (1980) *Environment, Ideology and Policy*, Basil Blackwell, Oxford.

best-known prophets of doom were the authors of *The Limits to Growth*, whose computer models led them to conclude:

> If the present growth trends in world population, industrialisation, pollution, food production and resource depletion continue unchanged, the limits to growth on this planet will be reached sometime within the next 100 years. The most probable result will be a rather sudden and uncontrollable decline in both population and industrial capacity.[3]

To reach such alarming conclusions, Dennis Meadows and his team at the Massachussetts Institute of Technology (MIT) constructed a series of 'World Models' based on relationships between population, pollution, non-renewable resources, industrial production and food supply, and ran them under a large number of different assumptions. In all cases continued growth led to 'overshoot and collapse' within the space of a few generations (Fig. 1.2). Imminent catastrophe is very newsworthy: *Limits* sold millions of copies worldwide and generated heated debate.

Critics were swift to point to serious limitations in the structure, assumptions and database of the models. In particular they accused the MIT team of 'Malthusian reasoning'[4] in their assumptions about exponential growth and finite resources. Technological progress, for example, was included only in single, discrete steps in the models. It was easy for critics to demonstrate that incorporating continuous, incremental progress (such as a 2% per annum rate of natural resource discovery), or social and economic feedback (for example spending more on pollution control whenever pollution increased), could postpone collapse indefinitely. Of course the *rate* of technological progress would have to be similar to the growth rates of population and consumption, but many technological optimists maintained that this had always been the case in the past and saw no reason to doubt its

Fig. 1.2 Results of the standard run of the World Model used in *Limits to Growth*, suggesting global catastrophe during the 21st century.

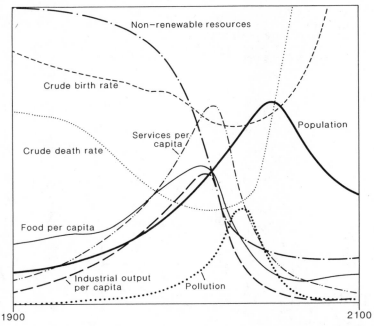

Source: Adapted from **Meadows, D.** *et al*. (1972) *The Limits to Growth*, University Books, New York.

continuity in future. Some envisaged a future of great plenty, if only people would allow technology and 'the market' to get on with the job. One contributor to a book entitled *The Resourceful Earth*, for example, could see

> . . . no barriers to a bright future for mankind . . . many minerals will eventually become more scarce and expensive, but we can develop substitutes for them. Food supply and environmental difficulties may well develop, but they can be solved. The only thing we need to handle these problems is an abundant and everlasting supply of cheap energy, and it is readily available in nuclear reactors, including the breeder. Given a rational and supportive public policy, science and technology can provide not only for the twenty-first century, but for ever.[5]

Even if growth were physically possible, however, there was still the argument that it was not *desirable*. In more affluent countries, the debate focused on the desirability of further economic growth – conventionally measured in terms of Gross National Product (GNP, the flow of final goods and services in the economy) – with many environmentalists maintaining that the social and environmental costs of growth had begun to outweigh its benefits. Paul Ehrlich, one of the key figures in the debate about growth and resources, was a well-known proponent of this view:

> It is clearly possible to reach a point where the gain in well-being associated with producing more material goods does not compensate for the loss in well-being caused by environmental damage. Beyond that point, pursuing increased prosperity merely by intensifying technological activity is counterproductive.[6]

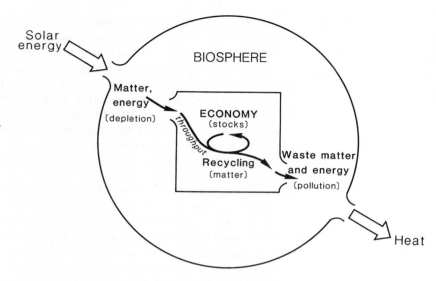

Fig. 1.3 The 'steady state economy', as envisaged by a number of authors, would minimise the human impact on the biosphere by minimising the throughput of energy and materials in the economy.

The anti-growth economist E.J. Mishan put it more succinctly:

> . . . the continued pursuit of economic growth by Western societies is more likely on balance to reduce rather than increase social welfare.[7]

The alternative to growth favoured by environmentalists was the 'steady state economy', in which population and capital would be maintained at near constant levels, and the throughput of energy and raw materials would be minimised (Fig. 1.3). The idea was developed by a number of authors who postulated a range of political, legal and fiscal means by which equilibrium might be established and maintained. A British version was published by the *Ecologist* magazine, one of many new environmental journals, in 1972.[8] This 'Blueprint for Survival' presented an 'orchestrated plan' for profound change to the social and spatial structure of the United Kingdom, culminating after one hundred years in a sustainable, steady state economy with a total of 30 million people dispersed in small, quasi-self-sufficient communities. In retrospect, 'Blueprint' seems both radical and naive; at the time its basic principles were endorsed by many distinguished scientists. Even *The Times*, in an editorial entitled 'The Prophets may be Right', argued that the case made by the environmentalists was 'too plausible to be dismissed'.[9]

Advocates of the steady state insisted that theirs would be a more satisfying as well as a more sustainable society: much of their writing embodies a strong anti-materialist ethic. In the brave new world envisaged in 'Blueprint for Survival', 'deserts of commerce and packaged pleasure would disappear' and there would be much less emphasis on 'shoddy utilitarian consumer goods'. Instead:

> . . . the arts would flourish; literature, music, painting, sculpture and architecture would play an ever greater part in our lives.[8]

It is easy to see why the environmental movement was frequently accused of being elitist, or even, as the then Labour Cabinet Minister, Anthony Crosland, once claimed, of having a 'manifest class bias' and is unequivocal on this point:

> Whilst it is true that there can be no sound environmental policy unless, at the same time, there is progress on the economic and social front, it is equally true that there can be no lasting economic and social progress unless environmental considerations are taken into account . . . environmental protection improves the quality of life and safeguards natural resources, thus permitting full realisation of the benefits of economic activity, in the form of better patterns of economic growth and employment.[14]

In other words, care of the environment is a prerequisite for growth – a stark contrast indeed to the anti-growth imperative of *The Limits to Growth* and 'Blueprint for Survival'!

The alacrity with which sustainable development (or 'green growth') has been adopted in policy statements is perhaps because it seems to offer the best of both worlds. Of course it does not. The message is that economic development is still possible – indeed essential – but as the *World Conservation Strategy* argues, it *must* be 'enmeshed within the possibilities and restrictions imposed by energy, chemicals and materials cycles'. Ultimately, therefore, these restrictions represent 'limits' to growth. In the meantime, rhetoric and practice are often two different things: much current economic activity is *not* sustainable and conflicts both with environmental objectives and with the potential for further development. Even 'green growth' would involve costs and benefits distributed unevenly in time and space, and would certainly not be free of environmental conflict. Some environmentalists still believe that genuinely sustainable development will only be achieved after fundamental social, economic and political change (see Chapter 7).

Few would deny that enormous progress has been made during the past two decades. Environmental consciousness is at a new level, and the crude conflict of the early environmental debate has given way to increasing consensus about the need for sustainable economic development. But defining and achieving sustainability presents a major challenge. Some fundamental conflicts remain, and both old and new environmental problems continue to prove resistant to resolution. Some of the factors that make these problems so difficult to resolve are considered in the next chapter.

2 Environmental problems and policies: some fundamental issues

I can't put a value on a meadowful of flowers or a wood filled with birdsong. *David Bellamy*[1]

Environmental problems at all scales – from the purely local to those with long-term global significance – raise certain fundamental issues which make their resolution difficult and contentious. Frequently-recurring themes, many of them interrelated, include the following:

- The intangible nature of many environmental 'goods' (the problem of *quantifying the unquantifiable*).
- The enormous *uncertainty* surrounding complex environmental issues.
- The uneven distribution of costs and benefits in time, space and society (the problem of social and intergenerational *equity*).
- The problem of distinguishing between *need* and *demand*.

The three case studies considered in detail later provide ample illustration of these themes. The purpose of this chapter is to draw the main issues together and to show why they have such troublesome implications for resource and environmental policies.

Quantifying the unquantifiable

One problem at the heart of environmental conflict is that not everything that people value can readily be costed in monetary terms. Activities that adversely affect the environment are typically defended in terms of quantifiable benefits like jobs and income, bigger profits, cheaper power or faster journeys. Some environmental *costs* can be quantified too, but many are uncertain, long-term or simply intangible, relating to cultural or aesthetic values. For example, pollution damage to commercial fisheries or loss of agricultural land for development has a calculable economic cost, but intangibles like wilderness, genetic diversity, traditional landscapes or ways of life do not. Yet it is exactly such 'fragile values' that have to be weighed against immediate and tangible benefits when decisions affecting the environment are taken.

Some economists argue that the only way to ensure that less tangible elements of environmental quality are not neglected in the decision-making process is to grasp the nettle and find ways of 'quantifying the unquantifiable'. David Pearce, for example, claims that techniques developed in economics have shown people's 'willingness to pay' for the environment to be positive and substantial. He argues that though such techniques are far from perfect, they should not be rejected by the environmental lobby because, for example, showing that wildlife preservation is worth millions or billions of pounds or dollars will be much more persuasive to policy-makers than simply recording some non-monetary measure of concern.[2] But others have been suspicious of

The beauty of an English woodland: can we put a price on such environmental intangibles?

attempts to ascribe monetary values to commodities that are never actually exchanged in a market, fearing that quantification may be used to obscure important value judgements in the decision-making process. This dilemma remains largely unresolved.

One major problem in trying to quantify environmental costs and benefits is that individuals have widely differing values and priorities, determined at least in part by the extent to which their various needs are fulfilled; their 'willingness to pay' for aspects of environmental quality will differ accordingly. The concept of a 'hierarchy of human needs' (Fig. 2.1), first developed by the psychologist A.H. Maslow, has often been cited to 'explain' why rich societies give higher priority to the environment than poor ones and why, even within developed economies, active environmentalists are most likely to be affluent, employed and middle class. Although we now recognise that environmental protection is as much a *basic* need as an aesthetic or spiritual one, much conflict, especially in developed economies, still revolves around the less tangible aspects of environmental quality – an unspoilt rural landscape versus development and jobs, for example. It is here that differences in values and priorities between different social groups make attempts at 'quantifying the unquantifiable' fairly meaningless (Fig. 2.2). In the final analysis, many environmental values are subjective and can only be asserted through the political process. Divergent social values will be found at the root of conflicts over control of acid emissions, exploitation of coal reserves and appropriate conservation policies in the Norfolk Broads, all discussed in detail in the case studies that follow.

Uncertainty

Environmental problems are often characterised by great uncertainty. The sheer complexity of the biosphere means that our understanding of the human impact upon it is very partial, and accurate prediction is often impossible. As knowledge advances, uncertainties are reduced,

Fig. 2.1 Maslow's 'hierarchy of human needs'. Maslow argued that needs of a higher order become important when more basic needs are met.

Source: After **Maslow, A.H.** (1970) *Motivation and Personality*, Harper and Row, New York.

Fig. 2.2 Development
and the environment:
conflicting values.

Development and the environment: conflicting values

One of the most controversial developments relating to the exploitation of North Sea oil and gas resources in the United Kingdom was a large petrochemical plant in Fife, Scotland. Shell UK and Esso Chemical Ltd applied early in 1977 to construct a natural gas liquids separation plant and ethylene cracker, together with a jetty and pipelines at Mossmorran and Braefoot Bay. What was interesting about this proposal was the totally different reaction to it in two communities equidistant from the site. In the largely middle-class and home-owning community of Aberdour and Dalgety Bay, opposition to the proposed development was vigorous, focusing on safety, pollution, despoilation of the coastline, effects on wildlife and restriction of public access to the shore. Nearly all of the objections to the application (there were more than 400) came from this area. In contrast, the residents of Cowdenbeath, a declining industrial community with high unemployment, welcomed the proposals for the employment and income which the development promised to bring to the area. Thus the same development and set of impacts on the environment can be viewed very differently by social groups with different sets of values and priorities. After a public inquiry, consent was eventually given for the Mossmorran plant in 1979 and it was subsequently constructed.

but they can rarely be eliminated. Problems like the 'greenhouse effect', for example, are so complex that society simply does not have the resources to gain a full understanding of the mechanisms at work on a time-scale with policy relevance. Often, as is the case with long-term effects of low-level radiation on human health, there is insufficient data to establish statistically significant relationships between variables. And some effects do not even manifest themselves until serious – and possibly irreversible – environmental damage has been caused; the bio-accumulation of the pesticide DDT and the formation and ecological impact of acid deposition (see Chapter 4) fall into this category. The crucial question is how environmental policies should be made in the face of such uncertainty. Must we wait for proof that harm is being caused, or should a more precautionary principle govern policy formulation? This has emerged as one of the key environmental issues of the 1980s.

Economic and social systems are equally complex. Uncertainty is inherent in projections and forecasts often used to justify policy

15

decisions with major impacts upon the environment; for example, assessments of the future need for coal based on assumptions about economic growth, fuel prices, markets for coal and future lifestyles (see Chapter 5). Projections based on past trends are particularly dangerous when underlying factors have changed. This is why UK energy-demand forecasts, based on observed relationships between energy consumption and economic growth *before* major changes in the world energy market in the 1970s, subsequently required substantial downward revision, though major investment decisions had been based upon them. There are considerable uncertainties in policy-making and implementation too: economic and social policies can have unanticipated and disastrous environmental effects (the Common Agricultural Policy is an obvious example), and policies aimed at environmental protection may have unforeseen social and economic consequences.

It is important to recognise that uncertainty is not merely an inconvenience that can be minimised or overcome with will and effort. It is inherent in all environmental issues, and we have to live with it, reduce it where possible, and above all acknowledge its significance. Uncertainty provides a good reason for caution and for erring on the safe side in environmental decisions; but in the political process it permits different interest groups to interpret data selectively and to promote courses of action that best suit their particular objectives. Nowhere is this better exemplified than in the conflict over 'acid rain', discussed in detail in Chapter 4.

Social and intergenerational equity

Costs and benefits that flow from environmental actions and decisions are incurred unevenly in space and time, and by different social groups. Any change (for example, sinking a new coal mine, or imposing controls on pollution) will result in a different *allocation of resources* within society; almost always, some individuals or groups gain at the expense of others. In economic theory the new allocation is 'efficient' if the 'winners' have gained enough to be able to compensate the 'losers' (whether or not they actually do so). In this sense, *allocative efficiency* means maximising *net* benefits in the economy. This concept is important because it underlies many techniques for evaluating the costs and benefits of new developments, including the costs and benefits of environmental policy itself. What matters in practice, however, is not only the *aggregate* result of change, but also its *distributive* effects. Whatever the proposal, the losers are unlikely to be philosophical about net gains to society as a whole and, whenever they can form a cohesive group, they are likely to present vociferous opposition to change. The case studies provide numerous examples of such reaction to resource and environmental policies.

Another important issue related to distribution is whether environmental policies have been *socially regressive* – that is, whether the losers have tended to be the less privileged members of society. This question has been debated extensively, but inconclusively. One view is that more affluent people benefit disproportionately from environmental protection because they attach greater value to environmental quality (according to the 'hierarchy of human needs').

Furthermore, articulate people can exert influence to protect their own immediate environment, sometimes at the expense of others; environmental campaigns have often reflected the NIMBY ('not in my backyard') syndrome rather than a broader concern with the degraded environments (such as inner-city housing estates) in which many poorer people live. There is some evidence for all of these claims. On the other hand, precisely *because* the poor live in the most degraded environments and are most likely to be exposed to environmental risks of all kinds, some policies – controls on traffic and vehicle emissions, for example – may benefit them more directly than the rich. It is difficult to generalise, because different environmental measures have different distributive impacts, but these should always be considered when alternative policies are evaluated.

The argument becomes even more complicated when the costs and benefits experienced by different groups in the present generation are weighed against those of generations yet unborn. What significance should we attach to the needs of future generations? Here we have to grapple both with uncertainty and with the concept of *intergenerational equity*. Most people, if pressed, express some sense of responsibility for future generations. But how should this be translated into practical policy? And how far into the future should it go – can we stop at our great-grandchildren, or should we consider people who will live in a thousand or even ten thousand years from now? Such time-scales are not unrealistic in relation to issues like radioactive waste management.

It is a matter of observation that individuals tend to value the future less than they value the present. Most people, if offered a sum of money now, or a sum *of equivalent purchasing power* to be received in one year's time, would choose the former option. They 'discount' the future. This notion is incorporated formally into evaluation of policies and projects, which always involve flows of costs and benefits over time, by applying a *discount rate* to future costs and benefits so that they are all expressed in terms of *net present value*. The use of any positive discount rate favours present generations; the higher the discount rate, the less relative weight is attached to future costs and benefits. The economist Geoffrey Heal, speaking in 1974, gave an interesting example of the 'destructive power' of a discount rate of 10%:

> . . . £100 in 1984 is worth only £37 today [1974], by 1994 it is worth only £13.50, and by the end of the century it is hardly worth having, at £7.42. Do you really believe that £100 to our children is only worth £7.42 as far as we are concerned?[3]

Costs imposed on future generations become similarly insignificant when a positive discount rate is applied.

The use of a positive discount rate was challenged as long ago as the 1920s, when the economist Pigou argued that disregard for future generations was the result of individuals' 'faulty telescopic faculty', which should be corrected by governments. In similar vein, many modern environmentalists have argued that a zero or even negative discount rate should be used to take full account of the needs of future generations. Others take the view that continued economic growth will mean that our descendants will be better off than us and well-equipped to look after themselves; after all, if resources had been 'saved' by our forebears for the current generation, we would not now be enjoying the fruits of the economic and social progress that was consequent upon their use. The real difficulty is that when resources are finite or destructible, and the basic needs of many members of the current generation are not satisfied, there must be some trade-off between generations. Intergenerational equity is a moral issue because our descendants are not here to defend their interests. It is hugely complicated by uncertainty about the future and by the fact that many of the costs and benefits cannot even be quantified, let alone discounted. The complexities are well illustrated by the question of depletion of finite resources, discussed in detail in Chapter 3.

Need and demand

Some of the most bitter environmental conflicts in recent years have arisen over facilities which are apparently 'needed' to meet some projected demand – coal mines for energy, reservoirs for water, motorways for traffic, and so on. Quite apart from the question of whether projections are accurate (they rarely are), there is an important underlying issue here concerning the definition of 'need'. In what sense is projected demand equivalent to 'need'? Should projected demand be met at any cost? Or should attempts be made to manage and control demand in order to minimise the environmental and other costs of new supply facilities? How should these choices be made? (Fig. 2.3)

Dire consequences of failing to meet electricity demand – as envisaged by the former Central Electricity Generating Board.

The philosophy that projected demand should be met has dominated planning decisions in both public and private sector organisations in the UK; indeed public bodies like the former Central Electricity Generating Board (CEGB), have had a statutory duty to meet demand. In the private sector (and increasingly in the public sector too) there is pressure to meet any demand which can profitably be met. ICI's justification for extending a mile-long limestone quarry face into the Peak District National Park in 1979 was that industrial demand for chemical-grade limestone would expand 'into the indefinite future' and must be satisfied. Similarly, the Opencast Executive (a semi-autonomous, and profitable, part of the British Coal Corporation) has resisted all questioning of the need for coal, arguing that need is determined by the market – this example is elaborated in the case study of the coal industry in Chapter 5. The consequences of failing to meet demand have generally been considered too awful to be contemplated.

It is of course extremely difficult to define 'need' beyond the most basic physiological requirements, but increasingly it is becoming apparent that meeting our material needs may conflict with our need for environmental quality. Inevitably such conflict raises questions about what we really require, and the relative importance of our different demands: these questions are prominent in all three case studies. A central issue is how far demand can be met before the development required to satisfy it becomes unsustainable. This is exactly the kind of area where it will be difficult and contentious to define what is meant by sustainability and it takes us straight back to the problems of uncertainty, quantifying the unquantifiable, and distributional equity.

Fig. 2.3   Projections of total primary energy demand in the UK made by the Department of Energy in the late 1970s and early 1980s. Should such demand projections be equated with 'need'? Note the *range* of projections, based on different scenarios, which provides another example of *uncertainty*.

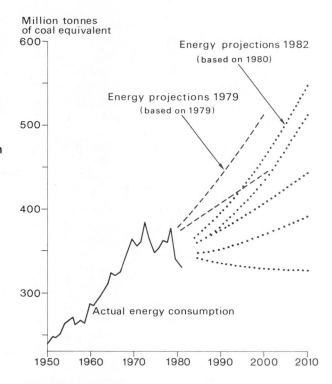

Source: Adapted from **Department of Energy** (1983) *Proof of Evidence for the Sizewell 'B' inquiry*.

The policy process

The issues discussed in this chapter mean that environmental policy-making is a difficult and contentious process. All too often this process is represented by a misleadingly simplistic model in which, once a problem has been identified as worthy of attention, its causes and consequences are analysed objectively by natural and social scientists and alternative solutions are explored. It is then up to the policy-makers, taking account of all the available evidence, to weigh up the implications for different interest groups and to reach an informed decision (Fig. 2.4). Once formulated, the appropriate policy will be implemented.

Fig. 2.4   The idealised environmental policy process.

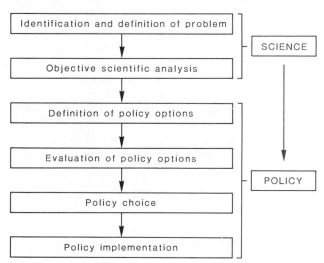

The realities of decision-making bear little resemblance to this pleasing model. First, science is never as divorced from policy as the model implies, and no analyst can be truly objective. One obvious reason for this is that organisations that conduct research have a far-from-neutral interest in the issue in question. In relation to 'acid rain', for example, the Chairman of the House of Commons Environment Committee observed that:

> . . . those scientists who seem to be supporting the energy generating industry take the view that not much damage is being caused, or the damage is caused by something else, whereas everybody else seems to take a different view entirely.[4]

But quite apart from specific loyalties, total objectivity is a myth because *all* analysts have values and preconceptions as a result of their social and educational background and the cultural context of the society in which they live. The very definition of problems, the questions that are asked in research, and basic concepts about legitimate goals in society (such as growth, technological progress or 'enterprise', etc.) are all essentially subjective. An analyst may conduct a cost/benefit analysis of alternative motorway routes, making a conscientious effort to exclude bias, but may at the same time take it for granted that a motorway is needed somewhere, and that an increasingly mobile society is a 'good thing'. Subjectivity of varying degrees, both conscious and unconscious, is woven into the whole process of policy formulation and implementation.

All stages of the process, including problem definition, are also subject to the influence of various interest groups and lobbies. Those who are most powerful generally wield the greatest influence. For example, during the drafting of the Wildlife and Countryside Act, the National Farmers' Union and the Country Landowners' Association were regularly and formally consulted by the Department of the Environment, so they were able to influence the legislation in its most important formative stages (see Chapter 6). Environmental groups were invited to comment only at a much later stage (except the Royal Society for the Protection of Birds, an earlier consultee). In a similar way, industrial interests have been closely involved in the formulation of pollution control policies. Environmental groups have not traditionally enjoyed the same level of involvement in policy-making and have had to pursue their interests in different ways and with rather limited resources. They are much more dependent on favourable publicity and the mobilisation of public sympathy for their cause, though sometimes these can be very potent weapons in the policy process. Some different models of the process of environmental policy-making are discussed in relation to resource management in Chapter 3.

All three case studies, together with the analysis of environmental progress in Chapter 7, provide examples of the often tortuous environmental policy process and the influences at work within it. All show how far removed is the reality of this process from any rational or comprehensive model.

3 Managing resources: some theoretical issues

The case studies in Chapters 4 to 6 illustrate resource and environmental issues at different scales. 'Acid rain' is clearly an *international* issue, but national interests have been crucial in determining the policy response to this problem. Exploitation of Britain's coal resources is a *national* resource issue, but it has significant local implications, both socially and environmentally, and is linked to the global scale through world markets and transfrontier pollution. The conservation of living resources in the Norfolk Broads must be achieved on a *local* scale, though the issue has wider ramifications because of the national importance of these wetlands. In resource and environmental issues, there is nearly always significant interaction between different geographical scales.

All environmental issues are essentially about the use and distribution of resources. Resources can be categorised in a number of ways, but one important distinction is between *stock* resources, which are (for practical purposes) fixed in quantity and therefore *non-renewable*, and *flow* resources, which are continually available, or *renewable*. Stock resources can themselves be subdivided into two categories: those which are 'consumed by use', such as the fossil fuels or the phosphate used in agricultural fertilizers, and those, like the metals, which in theory can be recovered and recycled. In practice, the potential for recycling is limited by technology and costs (especially energy costs), so that for the foreseeable future many theoretically recoverable resources will be effectively 'consumed by use'. Flow resources can also be subdivided, into those which are available regardless of human action (for example, solar radiation or tidal energy) and those which can be destroyed by unsustainable use (such as soils, forests or aquatic ecosystems). These categories are illustrated in Fig. 3.1. During the 1960s and early 1970s the prospect of 'running out' of many non-renewable resources on a relatively short time-scale

Fig. 3.1 A classification of natural resources.

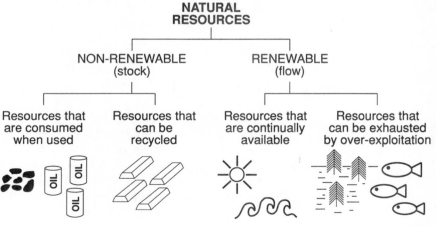

NATURAL RESOURCES

NON-RENEWABLE (stock)

RENEWABLE (flow)

Resources that are consumed when used

Resources that can be recycled

Resources that are continually available

Resources that can be exhausted by over-exploitation

caused considerable concern, but during the 1980s, as we have seen in Chapter 1, attention has shifted significantly towards the dangers of irreversible damage to the renewable resources of the biosphere. The case studies deal with both 'stock' and 'flow' resources, and also illustrate the relationships between them. 'Acid rain' is a product of burning non-renewable fossil fuels, but causes damage to flow resources such as forests, aquatic ecosystems and crops. Coal is of course a non-renewable resource, but its extraction and use has many impacts on renewable resources. The Norfolk Broads provide a case study of renewable or living resource management, and show how demands on such resources may be varied and often in conflict with each other.

This chapter provides some of the theoretical principles essential to an understanding of pollution, the depletion of non-renewable resources and renewable resource management. The case studies then provide examples of these issues and show how theory and reality are often rather different.

Pollution

Environmental pollution is amongst the most serious of contemporary problems, not only because of its immediate social and economic consequences, but because some forms of pollution disrupt complex biogeochemical cycles and may ultimately threaten the survival of the human race itself.

In this section we look at the concept of pollution and at some theoretical causes and remedies. In the real world, our response to the problem depends as much on political bargaining as it does on scientific evidence or economic theory. This is amply illustrated in Chapter 4, in which we consider the 'acid rain' problem, a major preoccupation of scientists, environmentalists and policy-makers in the 1980s.

What is pollution?

A widely accepted definition of pollution is as follows:

> The introduction by human action, directly or indirectly, of substances or energy into the environment, resulting in deleterious effects of such a nature as to endanger human health, harm living resources or ecosystems, and impair or interfere with amenities and other legitimate uses of the environment.

This definition raises some important issues. First it makes a clear statement about the origin of pollution. It is caused by people; sulphur dioxide from industry constitutes pollution, but sulphur dioxide from volcanic eruptions does not. When 'pollutants' are produced in nature, it may be difficult to isolate the effects of anthropogenic additions to the natural cycle.

Another important point is that pollution is deemed to occur *when damage is done*. Environments have some capacity to absorb and neutralise many substances, so a distinction is often made between pollution, involving harmful effects, and contamination, the presence of a substance in the environment below the damage threshold (Fig. 3.2). But this apparently simple distinction is problematic. In complex ecosystems we do not always know when damage is being done, and it

Fig. 3.2 Dose/response relationship with a 'damage threshold'. Some substances do not cause any harm (for example, to animals and plants) below a certain dose.

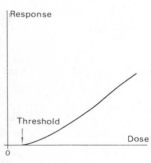

may not be recognised until it is irreversible. It has taken many decades, for example, for the damage to lakes and forests now attributed to acid deposition to manifest itself, and become a cause for concern. Contributing to the problem of time lag are substances like DDT or mercury, which accumulate in the environment instead of being dispersed and neutralised. As more information becomes available, it is often necessary for damage thresholds to be revised downwards. For some pollutants it is difficult to identify any threshold at all; for example, many scientists now believe that there is no 'safe' dose of radiation for human beings. The distinction between pollution and contamination is neat in theory, but sometimes very difficult to establish in practice.

The above definition of pollution begs one further important question: What constitutes a 'legitimate' use of the environment? Industry, agriculture, residential use, conservation and recreation are all legitimate; the problem is that they often conflict with one another. And whereas the benefits from some uses can be quantified, the benefits from others are intangible. It is not easy to decide what is 'legitimate' at any given point in space and time. This raises the thorny issue of conflicting demands on resources, an issue at the heart of all environmental conflict and well illustrated by the problem of pollution.

Pollution as an externality

Economists refer to pollution as a *negative externality*, a cost which is imposed on some members of society by others without compensation. If, for example, an oil refinery emits sulphur dioxide which ultimately damages forests and fisheries, the full costs of production are not paid by the industrialist, but are partly imposed on those who bear an economic loss because of the damage caused. It is possible to *externalise* costs in this way because environmental resources like clean air or clean water are *public goods*, or *common property resources*, discussed in more detail later. In the absence of controls they are effectively 'free', although they may not be in unlimited supply. If clean air has no price, industrialists have no incentive to economise on its use. In the case of the refinery, the atmosphere is used as a convenient free sink for waste. Oil products are produced at the plant more cheaply than would be the case if the full social costs of production were paid by the owners, so there is, in the language of neo-classical economics, a 'misallocation of resources' resulting from market failure.

This model may 'explain' why pollution occurs when the means of production are privately owned and producers have an incentive to maximise profits and therefore to externalise costs. But how then can we account for severe pollution problems in centrally planned economies where production has in theory been aimed at social well-being rather than profits? Philip Pryde,[1] in his study of environmental problems in the Soviet Union, suggests a number of explanations of which two are particularly significant. One is the 'primacy of production': in the drive to industrialise, production has been considered more important than other goals, and incentives and rewards reflect this order of priorities. The second is ideology: the view that the only source of value is human labour, so natural resources (land, water, etc.) have been considered free inputs to the production

23

processes. Although there is rapidly growing recognition in the Eastern bloc that environmental quality, as well as material production, contributes to human health and welfare, prevailing attitudes in the post-war period led to environmental degradation as inexorably as the profit-oriented market systems of the West.

If pollution is an external cost of production, the problem of pollution control becomes one of *internalising externalities;* for example, making industrialists pay for previously 'free' inputs to the production process, so that the full social costs of production are taken into account. There are several ways in which this could be achieved. In theory, 'victims' could negotiate directly (or through the legal system) with polluters to effect a better allocation of resources, for example by accepting compensation. In practice, the multiplicity of polluters and 'victims', uncertainty, information costs and the uneven distribution of power, make direct negotiation impractical and necessitate state intervention in pollution control. This could take the form of legislation to control emissions, perhaps specifying the installation of a particular kind of pollution control equipment. Costs would then be internalised in the form of pollution abatement costs, or penalties for non-compliance with the law. Alternatively, a charge or tax could be imposed on a firm according to the amount of pollution produced, providing a financial incentive for pollution abatement and/or resources to compensate those affected by the pollution. Another possibility would be to sell 'pollution rights'. There has been a great deal of debate about the advantages and disadvantages of different policy instruments for pollution control (see 'Further reading'); direct control by legislation has been favoured by most governments to date, though examples of pollution-charging systems can be found in an increasing number of countries including the United States, France, Sweden and the Netherlands. However, the choice of policy has more to do with practical and political realities than with theoretical minutiae. The foregoing argument strongly implies that the polluter should bear the costs of pollution control, or pay for environmental resources. The *polluter pays principle* has become a basic tenet of environmental policy. But in practice, as the acid rain case study shows (Chapter 4), it is not always easy to decide who is 'the polluter', and strict adherence to the polluter pays principle may have socially regressive effects (see Chapter 2).

How much pollution?

It may seem obvious that pollution control policies should seek to limit emissions so that the damage threshold in the environment is not exceeded or, for substances where there is no identifiable threshold, to eliminate emissions to the biosphere altogether. This approach is often urged by environmentalists, and we consider their argument below. But controlling pollution itself incurs costs. Typically, the *marginal control cost* (that is, the cost of controlling the next unit of pollution) escalates steeply as the level of contamination approaches zero (Fig. 3.3). Many people think that we should seek a balance between the costs to society of controlling pollution and the costs imposed on society if that pollution is unabated. This compromise is the *socially optimum level of pollution* (Fig. 3.4). For persistent or highly toxic substances, the optimum may be close to zero; but for many pollutants it would not be

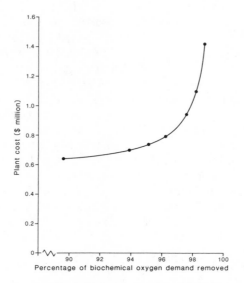

Fig. 3.3 Costs of pollution control. The graph shows the steep increase in cost as contamination approaches zero. In this case the 'contaminant' is biochemical oxygen demand (BOD), a measure of the capacity of an effluent to deplete water of oxygen.

Source: **Chemical Industries Association** (1983) *The economic case for defending the UK position on the control of water quality. The CIA view*. Chemical Industries Association, London.

zero because it would be 'cheaper' for society to tolerate some degree of pollution than to eliminate it.

In practice it is impossible to identify the socially optimum level of pollution. One major obstacle is that we have to recognise harm, and another is that we need to identify specific pollutants as the cause. The case of acid rain shows how difficult even these preliminary steps can be. Then, in order to draw the 'damage' curve, we must be able to quantify the damage done. This immediately raises one of the most important issues discussed in Chapter 2. Some effects, such as damage to forest or crops, *can* be quantified in money terms. But how are we to put a value on diversity in ecosystems, human health, cultural heritage or visual amenity? As we have argued in Chapter 2, any attempt to quantify such intangibles must be highly subjective. The pollution control cost curve, though often easier to plot than the damage function, also presents difficulties. Costs are not always known with

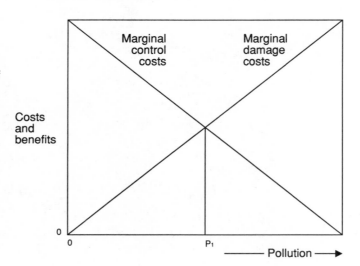

Fig. 3.4 The socially optimum level of pollution. This is the level (P1) at which the cost of controlling the next unit of pollution just equals the damage that it would cause. Marginal damage costs are of course the same as the marginal *benefits* to society of controlling the pollution.

accuracy, and will certainly change over time as technology develops. Nor should we forget that pollution abatement may have non-monetary costs too; for example, some methods of controlling acid emissions from power stations create a solid waste problem, and may impose intangible disruption costs on communities in the vicinity of the plant.

An alternative approach would be to try to eliminate pollution. Some environmentalists have argued that the benefits gained by polluting up to the socially optimum level (or whatever level is tolerated in practice) are being bought at the expense of future ecological stability.[2] This argument holds that in our present state of relative ignorance we should regard all pollution (some would even say all contamination) as a potential cumulative 'shock' to the environment which progressively undermines its assimilative capacity. We should therefore aim for zero pollution and regard the additional abatement costs as a kind of insurance payment. In begging the question, 'Who pays?' this concept immediately involves another recurring theme discussed in Chapter 2 – that of social and intergenerational equity.

Pollution control in practice

Since it is not possible in practice to identify a 'socially optimum' level of pollution, and since the objective of zero pollution is usually impractical (and encounters powerful resistance), pollution control policies are typically designed to achieve a level of pollution that is in some sense 'acceptable', often a compromise defined with reference to known impacts on human health or ecosystems. For example, national ambient air quality standards for major pollutants in the United States are set at levels designed to prevent both new impacts on health and aggravation of existing health problems. But what is 'acceptable' will change over time, and varies between different societies and within them. Levels of air pollution tolerated in cities during the industrial revolution in Britain would be unthinkable now; certain American standards for exposure to radiation are more stringent than British regulations; and the affluent may be able and willing to pay more for a pristine environment than the poor, who give higher priority to meeting unsatisfied needs for food and housing.

A tile-works before the 1956 Clean Air Act. What constitutes an 'acceptable' level of pollution changes over time.

26

The approach to pollution control varies considerably between countries. In Britain a pragmatic co-operative approach has been favoured, with emphasis on what is 'practicable'. Prosecutions for infringement of pollution regulations have been rare and fines relatively small. For example, potentially dangerous emissions to air have traditionally been controlled by the 'best practicable means' (BPM). Limits set for emissions from industrial plant by pollution inspectors (who have an intimate knowledge of the industrial processes that they regulate) assume that BPM is enforced, but what is 'practicable' depends not only on technology but also on considerations such as cost and other problems likely to be experienced by industrialists. In contrast, in the United States the system is more confrontational, with the courts being used extensively during conflicts over pollution. Emphasis may be on 'best available technology' (BAT) rather than on what is 'practicable'. When setting national ambient air quality standards, for example, the US Environmental Protection Agency was actually barred from considering the costs of their attainment. In some instances 'technology forcing' legislation has been implemented, involving the setting of standards (for example, for vehicle emissions) which must be met by certain dates, even if the technology needed to achieve them has to be developed in the meantime.

An important issue in pollution control practice is whether emphasis should be on the receiving environment (e.g. a river or the air) or on the source of pollution. Different environments have different capacities to absorb pollution, so if standards are set for the receiving environment (in terms of permitted concentrations of substances in water, for example), *discharges* could vary from place to place, depending on the *assimilative capacity* of the environment. A factory discharging an effluent into an estuary flushed twice a day by the tide could discharge more than a similar plant sited on the banks of a sluggish and already heavily polluted river. But for some substances, as we have already seen, the potential to cause harm in the environment is uncertain, so it is difficult to set *environmental quality standards*. And it is often argued that certain very dangerous substances should be controlled at source as stringently as technology reasonably permits; this implies the setting of *uniform emission standards*, regardless of the nature of the receiving environment. This issue is important because it has major implications for pollution control costs in different geographical areas: it has been at the root of a long-standing dispute between Britain and the rest of the European Community, described in Fig. 3.5.

One feature of pollution control common to all countries is that it tends to be *sectoral*. Air pollution, water pollution and disposal of wastes on land all tend to be dealt with by different agencies and different legislation. Sometimes this means that a pollution problem is transferred rather than solved; for example, reducing emissions to air or water may simply result in a solid waste problem. This is known as a *cross-media* effect. It is conceivable that tightening emissions controls for one medium could ultimately result in a worse overall impact on the environment. Ideally, all disposal routes should be considered and pollution should be dealt with in ways that minimise the impact on the environment *as a whole*. In 1988 the UK Department of the Environment proposed changes to legislation to achieve this, at least for

Fig. 3.5 Environmental
quality objectives or
uniform emission
standards?

In 1975 the European Commission published a draft Directive on Dangerous Substances in Water which proposed that discharges to water of 129 substances should be controlled at source by the same strict emission limits everywhere in the Community. The UK objected vigorously to these proposals, arguing instead for control by water quality objectives (permitted concentrations of the substances in the receiving water), which would allow *emission* standards to vary from place to place. UK industry, and the Department of the Environment, insisted that Britain's long coastline and fast-flowing rivers gave the UK environment a high assimilative capacity. If uniform emission standards were stringent enough to protect the Rhine and the Mediterranean, discharges from UK plants would have to be reduced to levels well below those at which harm could be detected. They saw this as a distortion of competition, with Britain being denied the benefits of the *comparative advantage* of a robust aquatic environment (compared in the dispute to the advantages of sunshine in other parts of Europe). The Commission and other member states, however, felt that a system that allowed variable emission standards would itself introduce unfair competitive advantages. This conflict – which has continued unresolved for fifteen years – is an excellent example of the interplay of economic and environmental concerns. On the one hand is the issue of competition, and on the other the question of whether there are thresholds of concentration below which even very dangerous substances can be deemed 'harmless'. The Directive has always been an uneasy compromise, allowing member states to choose between systems of control, and as a result little progress has been made. However, the UK Government has now accepted that certain toxic, carcinogenic and bioaccumulative substances *should* be controlled by the 'best available technology not entailing excessive costs' (BATNEEC), although the list is much shorter than that originally proposed by the EC.

more serious pollution problems, by adopting a more *integrated* pollution control policy.

It is crucial to recognise that there are conflicts of interest in pollution control. Any attempt to 'internalise' externalities will be resisted by those who have benefited from the 'free' use of environmental resources. Industrial interests, frequently with the co-operation of organised labour, have often been sufficiently powerful to delay the implementation of pollution control policies, to influence their formulation and even to evade them once they are enacted. This holds whatever the policy tradition of the country concerned; many examples may be found in the 'Further reading' suggested for this chapter.

If costs *are* internalised, they are likely to be passed on to the consumer. It may be argued, of course, that consumers of polluting products are in a sense 'the polluters', but the point is that such cost increases will be resisted, and they may be socially regressive (see Chapter 2). In marginal enterprises, increased costs may mean loss of jobs and, in extreme cases, the closure of a plant, with serious social consequences. Trades unions may then join forces with industrial interests to resist pollution controls, as was evident during the conflict in the 1970s over pollution from the London Brick Company's Bedfordshire works.[3]

It will never be easy to work out who benefits and who loses from different levels of, or different approaches to, pollution control. What is certain is that costs and benefits fall unevenly over time and space and between different groups in society. The development of pollution control policy is a political bargaining process, the outcome of which depends as much on the relative power of the various interests involved as on the results of scientific research. As the acid rain case study illustrates (Chapter 4), the notion of scientific objectivity becomes rather clouded when, in the face of genuine uncertainty, results can be interpreted in various ways and used as ammunition by different interest groups in the political process.

Transfrontier pollution

All of the above problems, serious enough in the national or even the local context, are greatly compounded when pollution crosses national boundaries. Costs and benefits then spread much more widely, the relationship between cause and effect becomes even more uncertain, and the victims of pollution have less power to influence policy than they might if the problem originated within boundaries where they have a political voice. As we show in Chapter 7, there are no effective means by which one country, acting unilaterally, can force another to reduce its output of pollution. The courts can and have been used, but international legal proceedings about pollution have proved costly, complicated and ineffective. International co-operation is clearly required and, as Chapter 7 shows, there is no shortage of good intentions to this effect, in the form of international principles, agreements and conventions. But states are only likely to take their responsibilities seriously if they are party to a binding international agreement which ensures that all signatories have to take similar measures. There are many problems in reaching such agreements, and in their implementation.

The international community is unlikely to settle on a comprehensive approach to environmental policy issues. Instead, the response to particular transfrontier pollution problems will be governed, like the response within national boundaries, by a delicate balance of interest and power. This is certainly true in the case of acid rain, discussed in detail in Chapter 6.

Non-renewable resources: some basic concepts

In this section, important issues relating to the production, distribution and use of non-renewable resources (metals and minerals, including fuels) are addressed. Given the historical significance of these resources and the dependence of the world economic system upon them, we would expect to find a substantial body of theory concerned with their availability and distribution: aspects of this theory are dealt with here. But in the real world, conditions are very different from those assumed in the neat theoretical models. The divergence is illustrated by a case study of the British coal industry in Chapter 5, which demonstrates the issues, problems and constraints associated with the exploitation of one particular non-renewable resource in practice.

When a resource stock is finite a number of important questions arise which have stimulated vigorous – often heated – debate. How much of the resource is available? How much should be extracted now and how much saved for future generations? And does the prevailing economic system ensure that the resource is allocated in the optimal way over space and time? None of these questions can be answered definitively and, as is typical of resource and environmental issues, the surface does not have to be scratched very deeply to reveal fundamental differences of values underlying the debate. We can begin by considering the first, apparently innocent question, of how much of a given stock resource remains to be extracted.

How much is left?

One thing that can be stated unambiguously is that there is a finite amount of a given stock resource in the Earth; this amount is usually referred to as the *resource base*, or 'total resources'. Its accurate measurement is impossible, though some crude attempts have been made to estimate the total stock of elemental minerals as the product of their 'elemental abundance' (in grams per tonne of crustal rock) and the known weight of the Earth's crust (sometimes to a specified depth). Such calculations imply that stocks are unimaginably large, but are fairly meaningless in terms of ultimately recoverable resources. The concentration of most elements in the Earth's crust (or the continental crust) is very much smaller than that in commercially valuable ores from which they are currently extracted. For example, the amount of copper in the Earth's crust estimated as above is enormous, but to recover one tonne of copper from silicate minerals in the continental crust would require the processing of 20,000 tonnes of rock; to recover one tonne of gold would mean processing 285 million tonnes of rock. Given the environmental and political problems associated with spoil disposal, and the energy requirements of this amount of processing, it can hardly be regarded as a serious proposition. The total stock of non-elemental resources (e.g. fossil fuels and ore deposits) cannot be estimated from 'crustal abundance'. Instead estimates have to be based on geological data, statistical analysis of trends in discovery, and actual exploration.

The resource base can be subdivided in a number of ways into categories reflecting varying degrees of certainty about recoverability. One such classification is shown in Fig. 3.6. *Reserves* are identified

Fig. 3.6   The resource base and its subdivisions.

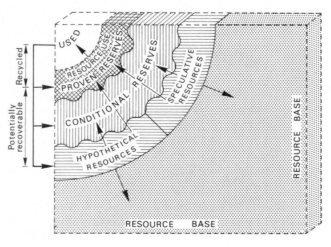

Source: **Rees, J.** (1985) *Natural Resources*, Methuen & Co., London.

30

resources of economic value, sometimes divided into *proven reserves*, which can be extracted at current prices and with existing technology, and *conditional reserves*, which are not economic under prevailing conditions. The boundary between conditional and proven reserves is subject to constant revision in the light of changes in market conditions, technology and government policy. Judith Rees identifies five factors that influence levels of proven reserves: technology, demand, production and processing costs, prices, and the availability and price of substitutes.[4] These factors are complex, interrelated and highly variable.

It is important to understand that reserves represent only a small part of the total resource stock. Beyond this identified portion is the category of *hypothetical resources* thought likely to exist in known mining areas or oil and gas fields that have not been fully explored. Even less certain are *speculative resources* which might be discovered in areas of favourable geology where little or no exploration has taken place. Some classifications include a category of *unconceived resources*, referring to bodies of rocks and minerals not yet recognised as deposits with potential commercial value. (An example is sphalerite, the sulphide of zinc, recently discovered in fractures of coal in the Illinois Basin.)[5]

Given the enormous uncertainties involved, it is not surprising that estimates of all categories of resources – even reserves – vary widely. As the geologist Donald Brobst puts it, 'Reserves and resources are part of a dynamic system and they cannot be inventoried like cans of tomatoes on a grocer's shelf'.[5] But it is not only a question of *intrinsic* uncertainty and dynamic change. Estimates of resources and reserves are produced by different interest groups and cited for specific purposes. Far from being neutral, objective figures, they are open to interpretation, manipulation and dispute. Thus oil multinationals have often been accused of underestimating reserves to boost prices and profits and it has been claimed that American gas companies keep three sets of reserves estimates: one for tax returns, one for the American Gas Association, and one for internal planning purposes.[6] In short, the question of 'how much is left' cannot be answered unambiguously and is rarely even addressed with objectivity. Wildly different conclusions – and policy prescriptions – have been reached by people working with essentially the same basic data.

Are we 'running out' of resources?

In the early 1970s there was bitter controversy about resource use and policy between 'catastrophists', who predicted the imminent demise of industrial society, and 'cornucopians' who believed that technology could overcome all problems of resource scarcity. The debate reached its height after the appearance of *The Limits to Growth*, 'Blueprint for Survival', and similar publications, discussed in Chapter 1. Critics were swift to point out that the alarmingly short lifetimes estimated for crucial non-renewable resources in, for example, 'Blueprint', had been obtained by dividing figures for *reserves* by current (or even exponentially increasing) consumption rates, inevitably leading to rapid exhaustion. In practice, though physical or economic exhaustion of specific deposits certainly does occur, reserves of most minerals and

31

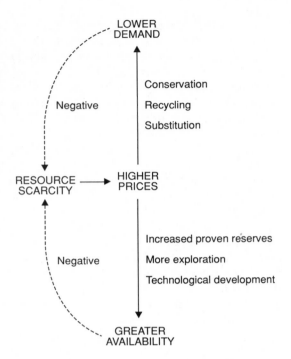

Fig. 3.7 The ideal market response to resource scarcity: in theory a negative feedback system ensures that resources do not abruptly run out.

metals have more than kept pace with consumption, and technological innovation has postponed the onset of diminishing returns as progressively inferior deposits have been exploited. There must logically be limitations to this progress, but optimists argue that they are too far into the future to concern us. By then, some cornucopians suggest, technology will have ensured that resources from elsewhere in the solar system are at our disposal.

The dispute really reduces to different perspectives on market response and technological progress. The classic model of response to resource scarcity is shown in Fig. 3.7. Scarcity (and anticipated scarcity) lead to higher prices which depress demand, increase supply and stimulate innovation. Problems of scarcity are either deferred as supply and demand again come into equilibrium, or become irrelevant as *substitution* occurs. Resource optimists believe in the efficacy of this process (sometimes claiming that it is limited only by government 'interference' and the power of organised labour). Pessimists tend not to share their faith in the market or in the inevitability of continuous technological progress. The 'limits' debate of the early 1970s involved extremes of each view, but these basic positions still underlie divergent opinions about resource exploitation. It is therefore worth considering the role of the market in the non-renewable resources sector in more detail.

Non-renewable resources and economic efficiency

According to neo-classical economic theory, a perfectly operating market in which individual private producers seek to maximise their profits would automatically result in 'efficient' exploitation of resources. More specifically, resources would be extracted and processed with minimum labour and capital input (technological efficiency); their production and use would exactly satisfy consumer demand (product choice efficiency) and the pattern of production would be optimal in time and space (allocative efficiency).[4] Unfortunately, the conditions which must be met to bring about this ideal state of affairs, including perfect competition, rationality, complete knowledge and absence of state intervention, are rarely, if ever, realised in the real world. Judith Rees, in a detailed analysis of this issue, argues convincingly that 'the minerals sector does not conform to any of the conditions needed to ensure that market forces will create economic efficiency'.[4] Furthermore, this situation is not a simple case of 'market failure', which can be corrected by state intervention, because 'the entire system is made up of inefficient conditions . . . inefficiency is not the exception but the rule.' The British coal industry, considered in Chapter 5, provides further specific examples of the failure to achieve efficiency of different kinds. Here we focus on the issue of *intertemporal allocation* – the question of how much of a given resource stock should be used in different time periods – to illustrate some of the points about the perfect market and the real world.

Optimal depletion rates

A question that received much attention during the 1960s and 1970s was whether non-renewable resources were being depleted 'too fast' (as many environmentalists believed), or too slowly. In theory the optimal allocation of a fixed resource stock over time is the one that maximises *net social benefits* (that is, the benefits of using the resource minus the cost of doing so). It can be shown that in a perfectly competitive market this optimal allocation should be the automatic outcome. At any given point in time, rational producers would extract a resource if they gained more (in interest) by selling the resource and investing the proceeds, than by allowing the resource to appreciate in value in the ground; in a perfect market, this behaviour should exactly cater for the needs of both current and future generations.

In practice, because of market imperfections, it is highly unlikely that non-renewable resources are being depleted at the optimal rate, though whether the actual depletion rate is too fast or too slow is more difficult to say. Monopoly control of resources, for example, would tend to make the depletion rate *less* than optimal because monopoly producers have an interest in making the resource last and in holding back supplies to achieve higher prices and maintain profitability. (Oligopoly, where the market is controlled by a smaller number of producers – OPEC, the Organisation of Petroleum-Exporting Countries, is a good example – can have a similar effect.) Overestimation of future prices by producers (who do not in practice have perfect knowledge of the future) would also result in too slow a rate of depletion. But other factors work in the opposite direction, tending to make producers 'discount' the future heavily (as described in Chapter 2), thus favouring the current generation. The general tendency to have a myopic view of the future and to plan production over relatively short time horizons would have this effect, as would uncertainty about the security of mineral rights, for example in a politically unstable country. When the 'dark forces of time and ignorance' encourage producers to adopt high discount rates, resources may be depleted 'too fast' (Fig. 3.8). A final example of a market imperfection is the existence of external costs, like pollution

Fig. 3.8 Resource
depletion and
intergenerational equity.

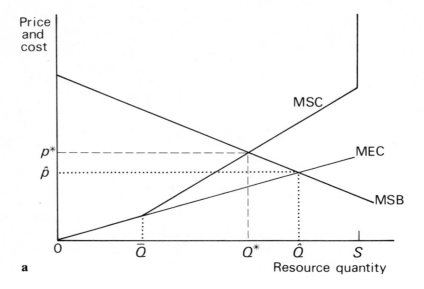

a

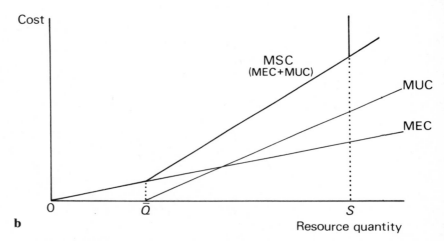

b

Source: from **McInerney, J.** (1981) 'Natural resource economics: the basic analytical principles' in
Butlin, J.A. (ed.) *Economics and Resources Policy*, Longman, London.

Notes: A resource stock (S), with only one use, is to be allocated between two discrete time periods,
t_0 (now) and t_1 (the future). It is assumed that society's preferences and extraction costs in each period
are known. Increased consumption of a resource will confer progressively diminishing *marginal social
benefits* (the more we consume, the less 'utility' we derive from the next unit of consumption), shown
as the downward-sloping demand curve MSB (Fig. 3.8a). The *cost* to society of consuming the
resource in the first time period has two components (Fig. 3.8b). The *marginal extraction cost* (MEC)
rises with increased consumption because of diminishing returns as inferior deposits are exploited.
At point $\bar{Q}$ the resource has been consumed to the point where what is left is just enough to satisfy
maximum future demand, so continued consumption is at the expense of the generation in time t_1. An
additional cost is then incurred by current consumption, equal to the (discounted) value of future
consumption forgone. This is called the *user cost* – an opportunity cost imposed on future generations
by current use. The *marginal user cost* increases with the quantity of the resource used now (MUC in
Fig. 3.8b). The true marginal cost to society of consuming a unit of resource in time t_0 is the sum of its
marginal extraction cost and its marginal user cost – this gives the *marginal social cost* curve (MSC)
shown in Figs 3.8a and b.
   Society will gain maximum net benefit from the resource stock when the discounted marginal
benefits and marginal costs of consumption are equal. From Fig. 3.8a we can see that this implies
consuming Q^* units of the resource stock in time t_0, leaving $S–Q^*$ units for consumption in time t_1. For
this to be achieved by the market, the price of the resource would have to be p^*. But if 'user costs' are
ignored and only *extraction* costs considered, more of the resource ($\hat{Q}$) will be consumed now, at a
lower price ($\hat{p}$). The higher the *discount rate*, the lower the present value of future consumption and
therefore the less significant the *user cost*.

from oil spills or land degradation by strip mining, which means that the true social cost of exploiting the resource is underestimated; the rate of depletion will then be too high. Those who believe that imperfections in the system reinforce the bias towards present consumption call for government depletion policies. But others argue that in the face of uncertainty the market is likely to do a better job than the state, even if the object of governments is to achieve intergenerational equity, which it usually is not! And, as noted in Chapter 2, not everyone agrees that rapid depletion is undesirable. In spite of much work and debate on this subject, it remains the case, as the economist Geoffrey Heal argues, that 'there are some very deep and difficult problems involved in deciding on the correct rate of resource depletion, and in deciding whether our own system is likely to achieve this'.[7]

In the real world, decisions about resource depletion are often not left to the market at all, but state intervention may be less to do with governments' concern for future generations than with more pressing and short-term considerations like regional unemployment, security of supply, or balance of payments problems. The case study of coal in Britain (Chapter 5) shows that extraction of this particular resource in recent times has had little to do with market forces and much to do with political and strategic factors.

Renewable resource problems and management

Following environmentalists' initial pessimism about stock resources and the finite nature of supplies ('limits to growth'), there has been, as we have noted above, a marked realignment of concern, with greater emphasis now being placed on renewable resource problems and management. Treated with care, renewable resources – which are capable of natural replacement on a human time-scale – might last indefinitely, but if destroyed, like the dodo they can never be re-created. While the prospect of 'running out' of non-renewable resources has receded, people have become increasingly disturbed by irresponsible exploitation of the renewable resources of the biosphere.

The continued health of the environment depends on how, and how quickly, renewable resources are used. Renewable resources need not be depleted provided that the rate of use is within the limit of regeneration and natural replacement. With that limit in mind, it is possible to use resources to obtain the *maximum sustainable yield* while at the same time ensuring continued supply. The essence of *sustainable development* is to guide processes of change in the environment by trying to keep exploitation of resources, technology, investment and institutional influences in harmony, thereby enhancing both current and future potential to meet human needs (see Fig. 2.1). If, however, demand and supply are thrown into disequilibrium and resources become over-exploited, depletion and/or degradation will lead to (perceived) scarcity. The whole gamut of environmental problems from global warming to changes in our immediate environment constantly remind us of the scale of effects on the quality and supply of renewable resources that have already occurred. In response, it may be possible consciously to manipulate, or manage, future availability by adopting a

35

sustainable development strategy, but just as with non-renewable resource issues, different individuals and groups in society are likely to bring their own interests and values to bear on the process. There will be many conflicting demands that cannot easily be reconciled. The poverty-driven destruction of the tropical rainforest versus the longer-term interest of the international community in a stable climate, cheaper electricity in one country versus healthy lakes and forests in another, and the amenity and conservation value of unique countryside like the Norfolk Broads against recreation demands and new farming methods, are just a few important examples. In the face of these incommensurables the supply of renewable resources ultimately comes to depend on the interplay of a whole host of political, institutional and socio-economic factors. Resource management is then an intervention mechanism through which different interest groups work out their relations with each other to determine the nature of available flow resources, how they are distributed temporally and spatially, and to whom.

What causes renewable resource problems?

As with non-renewables, population pressure, new technologies and levels of economic growth come high on the list of culprits accused of accelerating renewable resource depletion. Views soon begin to diverge, however, when the relative influence of each of these factors is considered, and on the question of what analytical framework offers the best chance of understanding the problem. Neo-classical economic theory and its shortcomings have already been introduced in relation to stock resources. Similar difficulties arise in applying this framework to flow resources, and need not be repeated here. It is, however, interesting briefly to reconsider the *externality* problem in this context. An externality is an example of market failure where, in the real world, the idealised model of perfect competition breaks down; the effect is to permit the costs (or benefits) of some activity to be passed on to others without those who gain from the exchange having to pay adequate compensation to those who lose. Sometimes the externality is positive, for example if the Forestry Commission fells trees previously obstructing a beautiful view from an adjoining property. But in the environmental field it is *negative externalities* that more typically give cause for concern. The renewable resource sector is a major recipient of negative externalities, the best example being the pollution that damages resources of the biosphere without producers having to pay (full) compensation for the harm done. As we noted in the earlier discussion on pollution, this state of affairs means that there is far more degradation than would otherwise be the case. We can now take this concept a little further.

Externalities are particularly significant in the renewable resources sector because of the problem of *common property resources*. An important assumption in the model of perfect competition is that everything of value can be individually owned, but in the real world this is not the case because there are numerous common property resources – the air we breathe and nature reserves, for example – that belong to everyone. The problem is that this can lead to a situation where 'what is everyone's is no one's': people may see no point in limiting their own use of common property resources, because other people will still use them without restraint. The inevitable result is overuse of renewable resources. This concept was popularised by Garrett Hardin in his essay, 'The Tragedy of the Commons'.[8] Hardin sought to draw attention to the 'tragedy' by using a metaphor. He envisaged a medieval community grazing cows on common land where the number of beasts just met the *carrying capacity* of the land; fewer cattle would mean some grass going to waste, but more would result in overgrazing. Hardin posed the dilemma of one individual with cows grazing the common. If the commoner added one cow, most of the *benefits* – the value of the extra cow and its milk – would accrue to that individual, but the *costs* – the effects of exceeding the maximum sustainable yield and so beginning to overgraze the common – would be shared by all the commoners. According to Hardin, the individual would feel bound to add an extra animal: if he or she did not, others might do so anyway, in which case the common would still deteriorate and the individual would suffer the degradation without sharing the benefits. Hardin's 'tragedy' is that *all* the commoners would follow the same self-interested rationality, causing the common rapidly to be degraded so that everyone would be worse off in the end. Although there are many problems with Hardin's ideas, his work remains widely known because people can easily make the connection between his 'tragedy' and the obvious destruction of many renewable resources. Resource management is the process that tries to prevent such tragedies from occurring.

In the 'tragedy of the commons' there is a two-way relationship where each commoner can ignore the effects of his or her actions on the others, but can do nothing to stop them behaving in the same way. The exhaustion of some ocean fish stocks is a real world example of depletion of common property resources. But there is another type of externality that is in a sense more sinister, where one group of resource users is able to avoid the external effect of resource degradation by transferring the disbenefits to some other unfortunate group. Transfrontier pollution is an example of this type of problem. Hardin developed a second metaphor which helps us to understand the underlying issues. Here his essential observation is that there are unequal relations between different groups competing for access to renewable resources which enables a privileged and powerful group to transfer the external effect on to a weaker and less privileged group. Many people would find this situation offensive to their sense of natural justice, but Hardin made a different case. In his new metaphor, 'Living on a lifeboat',[9] he envisaged a lifeboat (a valuable resource) occupied by a powerful group and surrounded by a sea of helpless swimmers. What is to be done in this situation? According to Hardin, the swimmers must drown lest sharing the boat with them causes it to become overcrowded and sink or (even worse!) the swimmers, if given the chance, might overpower the boat and throw its occupants into the sea. Hardin's view is that those who presently gain from the exploitation of resources must preserve their position. This is partly because he does not believe that the decline in living standards for privileged groups – the developed world, say – implied by more equal shares for all, would be acceptable to them, but mainly because he sees a threat to those societies from any alteration in the existing balance of unequal relations. We may assume that Hardin expects to reserve his own place in the lifeboat, but as we shall see below, there is an alternative way of looking at these issues. First there is one other important variation of the common property resource problem to consider.

Multipurpose resources, such as a national park which is a living and working environment as well as a refuge for wildlife and an area for recreation, often present problems because there is a 'halfway house' between common property resources and absolute ownership. A typical example would be agricultural land which a farmer owns outright, but through which an extensive footpath network gives the public unfettered right of access. Particular problems can arise when one group of users of a resource wants the owner to forgo the opportunity to use it in some particular way which reduces its utility to them. A farmer may wish to drain marshland, for example, to make it capable of growing high-yield arable crops, but meet opposition from conservationists arguing the importance of maintaining diverse semi-natural ecosystems and preserving a landscape which they perceive to have intrinsic value. Resource use conflict of exactly this kind has arisen in the Norfolk Broads and is discussed in detail in Chapter 6.

Renewable resource management

Although economics is vital to understanding resource problems, there are also political, social and ethical elements. In practice, these elements are so significant that they dominate the process of resource management as a means of resolving conflicts among resource-using groups. In a sense, the notion that renewable resource exploitation is about the competitive behaviour and conflicting interests of different groups simply adds a specific edge to the age-old ideological divide between rich and poor, privileged and underprivileged, and those who are powerful and those who are not. In a general context, the prominent American liberal J.K. Galbraith has stated the issue with disarming eloquence. (Should he ever take a trip in a lifeboat with Garrett Hardin they may find much to talk about.)

> Few things have been more productive of controversy over the ages than the suggestion that the rich should, by one device or another, share their wealth with those who are not. With comparatively rare and usually eccentric exceptions, the rich have been opposed. The grounds have been many and varied and have been principally noted for the rigorous exclusion of the most important reason, which is the simple unwillingness to give up the enjoyment of what they have. The poor have generally been in favour of greater equality.[10]

The ideological undercurrent revealed by Galbraith's stab at privilege has become very pertinent in relation to environmental problems, at least in sentiment if not in practice, and has found forceful expression through various calls for sustainable development policies. The most recent high-profile example can be found in the whole thrust of *Our Common Future*, the report of the World Commission on Environment and Development ('The Brundtland Report'),[11] which advocates the 'right' of people in less developed countries to higher basic standards of living. The report is openly critical of wealthier nations where, it claims, material aspirations are out of step with environmental capabilities:

> Perceived needs are socially and culturally determined, and sustainable development requires the promotion of values that encourage consumption standards that are within the bounds of the ecologically possible and to which all can reasonably aspire.[11]

The plausibility of this viewpoint rests in a strong moral appeal and it is no surprise that those who are losing out in the renewables sector frequently challenge the gainers in a high moral tone. Apparently rational objectives such as the maximisation of net social benefit, sustainable development and maximum sustainable yield are held to be virtuous alternatives to unrestrained fulfilment of self-interest. But as the above quotation makes explicit, resource management is not value free, and specific strategies may not always deliver their egalitarian promise. The 'rational' model of resource management (see Chapter 2) provides decision-makers with a cloak of scientific objectivity, but the truly subjective and judgemental nature of the process recommends caution when considering the arguments used to justify resource management policies and programmes. Thus it is always interesting to see who are the gainers and losers when renewables are distributed between competing groups and whether or not apparent objectives, such as maximising net social benefit, are actually achieved. We have already noted frequent criticism of environmental policy for acting regressively against underprivileged groups and protecting the interests and values of the middle class (Chapter 2). It is largely the middle class, for example, who have the inclination, education, time and income to enjoy the amenity value of the countryside, yet the conservation lobby has been quite successful in persuading the public sector to pay for countryside management. A more specific example can be seen in the way in which planning regulations constrain development in national parks, causing house prices to rise out of the reach of poorer groups who thereby have less chance to live in beautiful surroundings than they otherwise might. In fact, such policies make some types of rural housing into *positional goods* – goods in fixed supply that gain in psychic (and real) value precisely because they can never be available to any but a few.

Such considerations should not be misused, however, to argue against sound environmental policies. Rather, they show again that when considering the nature and distribution of environmental resources, it is necessary not only to seek public policy measures that might mitigate regressive effects, but also to consider the deeper issue of how and by whom the management strategy will be chosen and implemented, and who will pay for it. In seeking to understand the outcome of conflicts over multipurpose resources like the Norfolk Broads, it is important to understand how the decision-making process might work. We have already seen in Chapter 2 that decision-making is not necessarily a rational and comprehensive process and it can be quite revealing retrospectively to consider how closely managers' or politicians' actual policies compare with what they said they were going to do. This problem can be approached in a number of ways, but in this chapter we concentrate on two of the most widely debated ways to analyse decision-making processes, based on the concepts of *pluralism* and *elitism*.

According to the *pluralist* model the decision-making process is open, giving participatory access to the full range of competing interests. The openness of the process ensures that power is well distributed between all the groups because of the checks and balances built into the democratic system. Decisions must represent a consensus, reflecting public preferences, values and goals, arrived at during the bargaining process; otherwise they would not be generally acceptable and enforceable. The agencies that implement the policies can do so because they can argue that 'the public interest' is being served. *Elitism* is an alternative framework whose proponents stress the existence of elite groups – groups that are unrepresentative but able to distort the decision-making process because they enjoy disproportionate access to power and can mould policies in their own interests. There have been lengthy debates about which of these models most accurately reflects reality, but in practice elements of both models apply in many aspects of environmental decision-making. It is possible to detect both pluralist and elitist forces at work, for example, in resolving conflicts over the multipurpose use of the Norfolk Broads (see Chapter 6).

In a general context the very existence of environmental pressure groups supports the pluralist theme, but at the same time these groups frequently complain that they are at a disadvantage when challenging, say, the energy, transport or agricultural industries. Some would see these powerful interests as responsive to pluralist forces, but others point out that it is quite unusual for a pressure group to stop an environmentally undesirable development. It is much more typical for there simply to be delay (as with Sizewell – see Chapter 7), displacement (because of the 'not-in-my-back-yard' or NIMBY syndrome), or modification (for example, measures such as removing lead from petrol). These are concessions that can be seen as a process of *accommodation* in which the overall power and objectives of elite interests are not seriously threatened. It is also important to realise that despite undoubted successes, the issues taken up by environmental groups are only the tip of the iceberg. Most policies and decisions affecting the environment attract little publicity. Decision-taking is then effectively closed to public scrutiny, leaving the way open for a relatively restricted number of powerful interests to work out decisions amongst themselves, and that may include deciding deliberately to do nothing (non-decision-taking) if that is the preference of the groups involved. In return for privileged access to the decision-making process, each elite group will try to 'keep the lid on' the particular issue rather than bring it fully into the public arena, as pluralist theory demands. It is not difficult to see that the attraction for the powerful groups is the opportunity to shape decisions in line with their own interests. A notable example, taken up again in Chapter 6, is provided by the Ministry of Agriculture, Fisheries and Food which has often been criticised for defending the interests of a major 'client', the National Farmers' Union, rather than those of the general public who actually elect the government.

As Judith Rees has suggested, from a political perspective the key question is not how resource management decisions are made but who has the power to make them.[4] That is what determines the actual form of renewable resource management and the future of the biosphere.

4 Transfrontier pollution: the problem of acid rain in Europe

Acid rain is a classic example of transfrontier pollution. The term strictly refers to rain whose pH[1] has been lowered by solution of acidic pollutants, but it has come to be more widely applied to include acidic snow and mist, and direct (dry) deposition of acidifying gases and their gaseous and particulate derivatives. Acidic pollution originates from the combustion of fossil fuels (mainly coal and oil) and is often transported long distances in the atmosphere. Acid rain is widely believed to have a damaging effect on soils, surface water, forests, lakes, crops and buildings (Fig. 4.1). The phenomenon is generally recognised, but the precise mechanisms of atmospheric transport, acid formation, acidification of soils and surface water, and effects on ecosystems, are not fully understood. Such uncertainties are not purely scientific problems; they have important policy implications.

Fig. 4.1 The process of acidification.

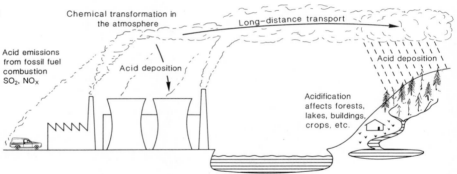

As with all transfrontier pollution, cause and effect are not only uncertain but are widely separated in space. Countries producing the pollution are not necessarily those suffering the worst damage. Canada, for example, suffers the effects of acid rain originating in the United States of America, and Britain's acid emissions contribute significantly to the problem in Scandinavia (Fig. 4.2). This spatial separation contributes to considerable political complications in trying to apply the polluter pays principle.

Origins of acid rain

Ironically the problem of acid rain originates partly in efforts made several decades ago to deal with severe local air pollution problems. After the disastrous London smog of 1952, when a temperature inversion combined with industrial pollution led to the premature deaths of 4,000 people, the British government finally felt compelled to introduce legislation to curb low-level air pollution in cities. One of the provisions of the ensuing *Clean Air Act* of 1956 was a 'tall stack policy'.

41

Fig. 4.2 An estimate of Europe's 'sulphur budget'.

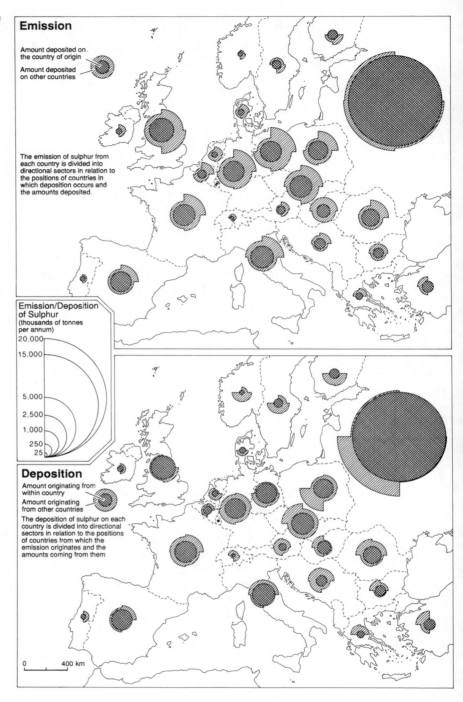

Source: Figures given by **Highton, N.H.** and **Chadwick, M.J.** (1982) 'The effects of changing patterns of energy use on sulphur emissions and depositions in Europe', *Ambio* **11**, 6, 324–29.

Note: Figures refer to sulphur, since sulphur dioxide is not deposited. Emission figures may be converted to sulphur dioxide from sulphur by multiplying by two. Estimates, especially for deposition, range widely, and the map can only provide an indication of the contribution of emissions in one country to deposition in another. Estimates are based on meteorological conditions prevailing in 1979 and 1980.

Since then the chimneys of power stations and other industrial plant have been built tall enough to disperse pollutants into the atmosphere rather than deposit them on the surrounding area. Unfortunately we are now discovering that the tall stack policy did not so much eliminate a pollution problem as shift it in time and space.

Acid rain is certainly a problem of anthropogenic origin. In the air over Europe less than 10% of the sulphur dioxide and about half of the nitrogen oxides (less near urban areas) are from natural sources. Sulphuric and nitric acids contribute to the acidity of rain in roughly 70:30 proportion. Sulphur dioxide emissions come mainly from industry, particularly power stations, and nitrogen oxide emissions come in about equal proportions from industry and from traffic.

The maps (Fig. 4.2) illustrate the very considerable geographical mismatch between emissions and deposition which is at the heart of the political conflict over acid rain. It shows also that with the exception of the Soviet Union, Britain remains the largest single emitter of sulphur dioxide in Europe, despite a 40% reduction in emissions between 1970 and 1984. British power stations whose emissions were not reduced in this period, annually emit about 2.8 million tonnes of sulphur dioxide – more than the *total* output in many other European countries. By virtue of its geographical position in relation to prevailing winds, Britain 'imports' relatively little transboundary air pollution but, in the view of the House of Commons Select Committee on the Environment,[2] is 'the worst polluter of other countries in Western Europe'. These factors have clearly influenced the United Kingdom's position in the conflict. In contrast, it is hardly surprising that the Scandinavians should be in the forefront of those pressing for urgent international action to curb acid emissions.

Effects attributed to acid rain

Serious damage to forests, fisheries and buildings, pollution of groundwater and suspected damage to crops, materials and even human health has stimulated mounting concern about acid rain in Europe since the late 1960s. In particular, the huge and widespread increase in damage to forests, especially in central and southern Germany, and the 'deaths' of many lakes in Scandinavia, have led to intense pressure for pollution control; in this chapter we focus on the impacts on forests and aquatic ecosystems. Inevitably, there are major conflicts of interest between the suspected 'polluters' and those who see themselves as most at risk. In the intense debate, two questions have emerged as being of crucial importance. Does acid rain *cause* the observed effects? And if so, would reducing acid emissions mitigate or reverse them?

Forests

> Forest damage in Europe is extensive, accelerating and of immense economic significance. In addition, other serious ecological problems may follow deforestation.

This was the view of the House of Commons Select Committee on the Environment (the Environment Committee) in its report on acid rain.[2] In West Germany, at least 50% of the forest area is affected, and in

Damage to trees by acid rain.

300,000 hectares of the Black Forest, every tree is damaged. Effects vary from species to species, but include 'dieback' of tree tops, discolouration and shedding of needles or leaves, death of branches and damage to bark. Actual death of trees is most likely to occur through secondary factors, such as fungal or insect attack, but death is usually pre-empted by foresters felling the trees first. Where trees are not cropped, the effects are dramatic. The Environment Committee report that:

> In the Black Forest we visited a hill-top which had been left in order that foresters might observe the effects of the damage if it took its full course. It was totally denuded.

What is causing the devastation? It has become increasingly obvious that there is no simple or single explanation, but the most widely accepted view is that air pollution in combination with other factors is responsible for the damage. Many of the forest ecosystems of central and southern Germany are naturally fragile because of altitude and acidic soils. Forest management practices, drought and insect or fungal attack have all been implicated as possible causes of the observed effects, but the spatial distribution of damage and its marked increase in recent years suggest that some other factors must be significant. At first it was thought that acid precipitation released toxic metals, especially aluminium, in the soil, and that these toxins damaged tree roots causing nutrient deficiency and making the trees susceptible to disease. This theory fell out of favour when damage was observed in areas where the soil is not acidic. The role of ozone (O_3) has also received attention. Ozone occurs naturally in the lower atmosphere in very variable concentrations depending upon atmospheric conditions. However, high concentrations of ozone are usually the result of the action of sunlight on pollutants such as nitrogen oxides and hydrocarbons. The gas has been shown to affect trees at relatively low concentrations. Levels are highest at high altitudes, and during fine, hot weather – all of which fits the temporal and spatial patterns of tree damage. Research suggests that ozone may predispose trees to damage by acid pollution (especially acid mists). Theories are likely to evolve or even to change radically as new evidence becomes available, but the current state of knowledge is summarised well in a report prepared for the Commission of the European Communities:

> It seems very probable that a major contributing cause to the . . . damage to forests in various parts of Germany is acid pollutant emissions . . . . However, geography, soil conditions, climate and possibly forest management practice are also undoubtedly important factors. The mechanism of visible damage to trees is by no means established, although there is increasing evidence to show that:
>
> (i) direct attack by pollutants/acid rain is probably more important than indirect mechanisms involving root/soil aluminium transfer mechanisms;
> (ii) apart from SO_2/SO_4 precipitations, ozone and possibly NO_2 are likely in many circumstances to play an important contributory (and synergistic)[3] role as damaging agents.[4]

If damage is due to direct effects of gaseous pollutants, it is more likely to be reversible following improvements in air quality. The longer-term stress theory, however, implies that older trees may not recover; if stress involves indirect effects through the soil, recovery even for newly planted trees may take decades because of storage of pollutants in the soil and the slow rate of replenishment of depleted nutrients from bedrock weathering.

Whatever the cause, many West Germans feel a sense of helpless outrage at the destruction of forests which are of immense economic, recreational and psychological significance to them. One estimate suggests that the direct economic loss may be of the order of £120 million per annum (some are higher),[4] and that 47,000 jobs in forestry and associated industries may be lost.[5] But such figures hardly begin to express the true costs. As Steve Elsworth argues in his book, *Acid Rain*:

> There is a sort of wooden stupidity about a cost-benefit analysis of a forest death . . . It is a Kafkaesque process, working under the rationale that a forest is worth the total sale price of its wood . . . [but] how do you put a price on the Black Forest? Is, for example, a 2 per cent loss per year merely another entry in the economic ledger, or an irreversible ecological catastrophe which could last for centuries and should be avoided at all costs? How do you cost the effect of a dead forest on the quality of life of the local community?[5]

Forest death is a very pertinent example of the problems of 'quantifying the unquantifiable', discussed in Chapter 2.

Scandinavian lakes

The other serious ecological problem in Europe that has been widely attributed to acid rain is the substantial decline in fish populations, particularly those of brown trout and salmon, in southern Scandinavia. In southern Norway, all lakes in an area covering 1.3 million hectares are practically devoid of fish, and fish stocks are reduced in a further 2 million hectares. In southern Sweden, aquatic life has been damaged in about 20% of lakes. As with forest damage, the economy as well as the environment suffers. The Organisation for Economic Co-operation and Development (OECD) estimates the value of the losses of fish alone to be in the region of $28 million per annum, but again this is hardly an adequate measure of the true cost of ecosystem damage.

The questions that must be addressed are whether the decline in fish populations is due to acidification, whether acid rain is a causal factor, and whether pollution abatement will help. None of these questions is easy or straightforward to answer.

There *is* evidence that surface waters in Scandinavia have become more acid during the past fifty years. Data from Norway indicate that pH levels in lakes have declined from around 5.5 in 1940 to current levels of 4.7. In Sweden, the pH of fifteen lakes on the south-west coast has fallen from the range 8.0–6.5 in the 1930s and 1940s to 4.5 in the 1980s. And a certain amount of evidence from sediment analysis in Sweden suggests an acceleration of acidification in the past twenty years.

The decline of fish populations has also been marked since 1940,

Fig. 4.3 Brown trout
population changes.

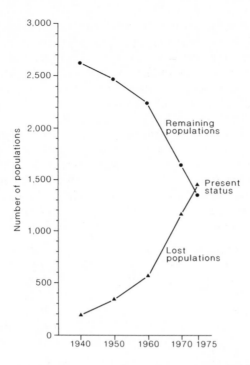

Fig. 4.3 Brown trout population changes.

Source: **Sevaldrud** and **Muniz** (1980) *Acid Lakes and Inland Fisheries in Norway. Reports of Interview Surveys 1974–1979*, SNSF Project IR 77/880, Norwegian Institute for Water Research, Oslo.

though losses have been observed since the beginning of the century (Fig. 4.3). The coincidence of the two phenomena – acidification, and decline of fish populations – obviously makes it a reasonable hypothesis that they are related, though as with forest damage, it is not easy to establish cause, effect and mechanism.

Acidification of surface waters is complex. Lakes can become acidified directly, through wet and dry acid deposition on their surfaces, and indirectly, through acidification of their catchment areas. Much depends on the geology of the catchment and the lake bed; some rocks, like sandstone or limestone, are effective 'buffers' (having a high neutralising capacity), but others, like granite or gneiss, provide no protection against acidification of the water. As the water becomes more acid, different organisms begin to disappear, and the end result is a greatly impoverished ecosystem. Fish may be killed because the pH becomes too low for their foodstock to be maintained, or, especially after acid 'surges' following spring snowmelt or heavy autumn rains, because the water is too acid for eggs to hatch, fry to survive or fish themselves to live. Aluminium, leached from soils in the catchment by acidic precipitation, is highly toxic to fish, and is thought to play a key role, especially in the absence of calcium. Although the mechanisms are not all fully understood, pH, calcium levels and aluminium levels are all thought to be important interacting factors in the survival of fish populations.

Unfortunately, available data showing acidity levels and fish populations *over time* are inadequate to demonstrate a clear relationship. An alternative approach is to attempt to correlate the two variables for a sample of different lakes at any one point in time – that is, a 'cross-sectional' method. The Sorlandet Lake Area in southern Norway has been closely studied in this respect; it includes more than 3,700 lakes, which vary considerably in size and catchment area. When controlled for the buffering capacity of catchments, analyses have indicated a relatively strong correlation between fish population and pH, suggesting that the decline of fish populations *is* related to acidification.

It remains to be shown whether acid rain is responsible for the acidification of lakes. Could the changes be due to other human activity or to natural processes? One possible culprit was thought to be afforestation. It is known that forests, especially coniferous forests, tend to increase the acidity of rainfall as it passes through the tree canopy. Soils may become acidified, especially if the trees are cropped, removing the alkalis which in a natural cycle would return to the soil. But acidification of lakes in Scandinavia was first observed above the tree line, and research in Galloway, Scotland (an area of Britain that is susceptible to acidification) found that lakes that did not have forested catchments were acidified. In any case, the acid deposition collected by the trees must come from somewhere!

Another hypothesis about lake acidification is that it is primarily due to changing patterns of land use, particularly the fact that transhumance is no longer practised in lake catchments. This view is not widely held, but one of its main proponents, Professor Ivan Rosenqvist, figured prominently in a video film on acid rain produced by the British Central Electricity Generating Board (CEGB) in 1985. This so incensed the Norwegians that it provoked a diplomatic protest to the effect that the truth was being 'distorted' by the way in which scientific opinions were presented in the film. The 'land use change view' has been countered by Dr Rick Battarbee and his colleagues at University College London, who have analysed diatoms in lake sediments in Galloway, Scotland. Diatoms are tiny algae which are very sensitive to acidity, so the presence or absence in sediments of the skeletons of particular types of diatoms is a good indicator of the acidity of the environment at different times. Battarbee's research found that the lakes in Galloway (a granite area) have become sharply more acidic in the past century, and that the sudden change coincided with the onset of industrial air pollution (Fig. 4.4). The National Coal Board was even able to identify some of the soot particles found in the lake sediments as originating in particular coalfields! Industrial pollution, rather than major catchment change, is strongly implicated in the acidification of these lakes.

In summary, there is evidence but not absolute proof, that acidification of water damages aquatic life; that lakes in southern Scandinavia have become increasingly acid over the past thirty years; and that acid precipitation contributes to this problem. Other factors, including afforestation, acid soil and slow-weathering geology, are almost certainly involved, but in the view of the Environment Committee, 'Without acid deposition, none of these factors would cause the scale and suddenness of damage to aquatic life being observed now.'[2] Once again, there is considerable uncertainty about the extent to which damaged lakes could recover their pH levels, buffering capacities and fish populations if pollution were reduced; if damage is irreversible, controls are arguably more urgent, because lakes not yet acidified may be saved.

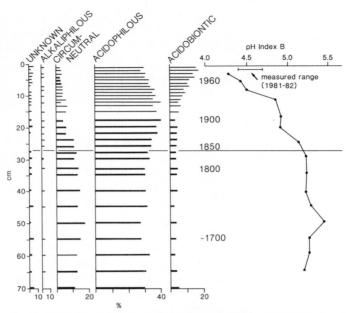

Fig. 4.4 Diatoms in Loch Enoch, Galloway. The diagram shows a shift towards more acid-loving species such as the acidobiontic *Tabellaria binalis* since the mid-19th century.

Source: **Environmental Data Services Ltd,** Report 132 January 1986. Original work by R. Battarbee. Reprinted by permission from *Nature* **314**, no. 6009, pp. 350–52, 28 March 1985 © 1985 Macmillan Magazines Ltd.

Some important uncertainties

As the forest and lake examples demonstrate, substantial uncertainties remain about the processes through which damage occurs, and about their reversibility. It is difficult to predict how far ecosystems would recover if acid deposition were reduced. But it is also far from certain that a reduction in acid *emissions* would lead to a proportionate reduction in *deposition*. Some scientists believe that the formation of acid rain is limited by meteorological conditions and by the availability of other chemicals – hydrocarbons, for example – so that not all of the available sulphur dioxide is converted. This is crucial, for if the limiting factor is *not* sulphur dioxide, but atmospheric conditions or another chemical, then it follows that reducing *emissions* may not proportionately reduce the amount of acid rain that falls. Given its important policy implications, the 'linearity issue', as this problem has been called, has been hotly debated, but remains substantially unresolved.

The policy dilemma

A report prepared for the Commission of the European Communities summed up the situation as follows:

> . . . circumstantial evidence would suggest that acid emissions and their subsequent chemical transformation and precipitation are at least a partial contributory cause of [the] observed effects [on forests, lakes, etc.] and may be giving rise to as yet unidentified impacts, some of which could be irreversible, [but]
> . . . it has not been *unequivocally established* that these environmental impacts are caused by acid pollutant emissions, nor is the relative importance of other factors properly identified.

. . . considerable further investigations are required to understand the mechanisms involved.[4] (Author's emphasis)

Such uncertainty clearly presents a policy dilemma. Should immediate action be taken, in the absence of 'proof', because of the serious risk of irreversible damage to ecosystems? Or should pollution control – which will be expensive – wait upon the results of further research, while damage continues?

The positions adopted by different interests in this debate reveal much about the relationship between science and policy in complex environmental problems. Contrast, for example, the views of the environmental pressure group Friends of the Earth (FOE) with those of the Confederation of British Industry (CBI), both given in evidence to the House of Commons Select Committee on the Environment.[2] While FOE argued that:

> . . . sulphur emissions must be reduced in the short term rather than the long term to prevent further acidification and to begin the slow process of restoring the damaged areas. The reduction . . . cannot wait until further refinement of the mathematical models,

the CBI maintained:

> Whether reduction of SO_2 emissions will . . . lead to an acceptable solution of the 'acid deposition' issue is highly dubious. It is premature and unwise to make costly legislative demands when considerable resources are being expended on the problem and on possible solutions.

Lord Marshall, Chairman of the Central Electricity Generating Board (CEGB), defended a similar position to the Committee on the grounds that:

> . . . we might spend a lot of money and then find that the effect is negligible . . . We are not procrastinating . . . We are just trying to do our conscientous job as we see it.

Broadly speaking, environmentalists and the 'victims' stress the ecological risks; 'polluters' emphasise uncertainties and costs.

Costs of emission controls

As with all pollution control, the reduction of acid emissions incurs costs. The CBI and the CEGB have argued that in the case of lakes it might be more cost-effective to treat the target rather than the source of acid pollution, by adding calcium to the water in the form of lime to reduce pH and lower the amount of aluminium in solution. In Sweden, 278 lakes were limed between 1977 and 1984, resulting in the recovery of some fisheries and enabling some lakes to be restocked. Loch Fleet, a small acid lake in Galloway, Scotland is receiving similar treatment. But the consensus of opinion is that liming is a short-term emergency measure rather than a long-term practical solution. Apart from problems related to the sheer number and inaccessibility of affected lakes, it can hardly be prudent to mitigate one ecological problem in a way that could well lead to others. No equivalent measure has been

identified to reverse, even temporarily, the damage to forests.

This leaves the reduction of emissions as the only viable long-term option for dealing with acid pollution. There are a number of ways in which this could be done, which are summarised in Fig. 4.5. Making a transition from fossil fuels to nuclear or renewable sources represents a long-term (and controversial) solution. Using energy more efficiently certainly has a very important role to play. But for the foreseeable future the combustion of fossil fuels on a large scale in power generation, industry and vehicles will continue and if there is a need for pollution control, attention must be directed at these sources.

The most practical and immediately available options for controlling acid emissions are flue gas desulphurisation (FGD) – filtering emissions in power station or factory chimneys to remove up to 95% of the sulphur dioxide – and the installation of low nitrogen oxide burners. Nitrogen oxide (and other) emissions from vehicles can be reduced by catalysts and (though this technology is not fully developed in 1990), by 'lean-burn engines' in which virtually total combustion of the fuel takes place. Both FGD and vehicle catalysts are known technologies which have been in use for some time in Japan and the United States.

Cost estimates vary and are likely to change as technology develops, but installing FGD in a large power station (2,000 megawatts (MW)) is likely to cost several hundred million pounds, with costs being rather larger for 'retrofit' than for a new power station; annual running costs will be in the order of £20 million. It is estimated that retrofitting FGD to 12,000MW of UK generating capacity (which might be necessary to meet the requirements of new European legislation, discussed below) would cost an initial £1.8 billion, incur annual running costs in the order of £120 million, and add 2% to electricity bills. For vehicles, 'three-way catalytic converters', also required by European legislation by the early 1990s, are likely to add £400–£600 to the cost of a new car.

Although there is not complete agreement about the costs of reducing emissions from industry and motor vehicles, it can hardly be denied that they are substantial. It is likely that they will be passed on to the consumer, and since consumers of electricity or cars are, in a sense, polluters, this could be seen as a proper application of the polluter pays principle (see Chapter 3). But there are two problems, involving

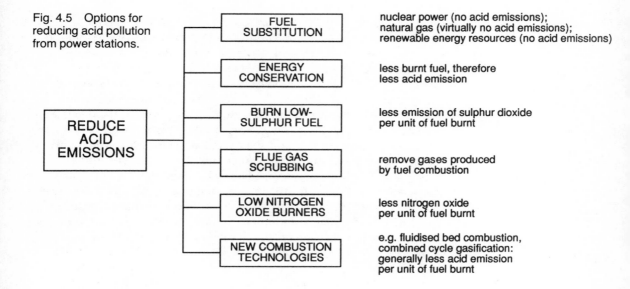

Fig. 4.5 Options for reducing acid pollution from power stations.

REDUCE ACID EMISSIONS

FUEL SUBSTITUTION — nuclear power (no acid emissions); natural gas (virtually no acid emissions); renewable energy resources (no acid emissions)

ENERGY CONSERVATION — less burnt fuel, therefore less acid emission

BURN LOW-SULPHUR FUEL — less emission of sulphur dioxide per unit of fuel burnt

FLUE GAS SCRUBBING — remove gases produced by fuel combustion

LOW NITROGEN OXIDE BURNERS — less nitrogen oxide per unit of fuel burnt

NEW COMBUSTION TECHNOLOGIES — e.g. fluidised bed combustion, combined cycle gasification: generally less acid emission per unit of fuel burnt

issues of intergenerational and social equity. One is that current consumers are being asked to pay to clean up pollution caused by their predecessors and to ensure a cleaner environment for the future. The other is that those who can least afford it pay disproportionately for pollution controls unless there are compensatory social policy measures. Fuel, for example, accounts for more than 11% of the total expenditure of low-income households, compared with just over 6% for average households. Adjustments to the taxation or benefit system should occur if environmental measures resulting in increases in fuel prices are not to have a socially regressive impact. An alternative would be to subsidise major pollution control expenditure out of general taxation, but this would violate the polluter pays principle. However, in considering these general principles, we should not lose sight of the fact that cost increases (in the case of electricity) would be spread over a decade or more, and would be very small in relation to increases caused by other factors.

Cost increases for other industries (for emission controls and increased electricity prices) may also be passed on to the consumer, but marginal firms may shed labour or even go out of business; this too could have regressive social consequences. On the other hand, pollution control itself creates and protects jobs; for example, orders for FGD equipment for the Drax power station in Yorkshire have secured the jobs of 1,000 employees of the main contractor at a plant in Scotland. Pollution control may also incur indirect costs. For example, there are opportunity costs: if £2 billion is spent on FGD it cannot be spent on hospitals, education or other kinds of environmental improvement which might have more immediate and certain effects (much-needed investment to reduce water pollution from sewage plants, for example). In each case there are different sets of benefits and costs, enjoyed or borne by different groups in society. Finally, it should not be forgotten that acid emissions control has environmental impacts too. There are very large raw materials requirements (for example, limestone, which

51

must be quarried from somewhere), and although systems can be designed to produce commercially useful by-products, like gypsum, if the cement and construction industries cannot absorb all the extra material there are solid waste problems, with environmental costs incurred both at the land disposal site and along the transport route.

Against the costs of control have to be set the damage allegedly caused by acid pollution, and the benefits to be gained if the damage is halted and/or reversed. As we have seen, the damage to German forests and Scandinavian lakes imposes very considerable costs, even if only those that can readily be quantified are taken into account. But a detailed cost-benefit analysis can hardly be meaningful when so many of the benefits (and costs, for that matter) are intangible, and there are so many uncertainties about exactly *whose* pollution is causing precisely which effects. To take one example, it is impossible to predict with any certainty how a reduction in British sulphur dioxide emissions in line with the European Community's Large Combustion Plant Directive (discussed below) would change the acidity or fish population of Norwegian lakes, let alone to try to quantify the costs and benefits involved. There *is* evidence that controls on acid pollution would be cost effective in broad terms; an OECD study suggested that for an annual cost of around £730 million, Western Europe could achieve monetary benefits, excluding many intangibles, of £520–£4,600 million. But as the Natural Environment Research Council argues, 'the issue really depends upon what emphasis the population place upon their environment'.[2] In other words, the 'socially optimum level' of acid emissions is an elusive concept indeed. It is very interesting, in these circumstances, to see how compromise solutions are slowly developed in the environmental policy-making process.

Environmental politics

Countries affected by acidification began to exert pressure on the international community when serious impacts manifested themselves in the 1970s, but with little effective power they made virtually no progress. A conference on acid rain in Stockholm in 1982 marked a major shift in the debate when West Germany, one of the principal polluters, changed position abruptly and announced stringent unilateral controls on acid emissions. This volte-face, due in part to increasingly obvious damage to German forests and in part to the growing influence of the 'Greens' in German politics, had two significant effects. It changed the situation within the European Community, where the Germans now began to use their powerful position to press for Community-wide pollution control, so that German industry would not be placed at a competitive disadvantage by the new measures; moves were initiated which led eventually to the Large Combustion Plant Directive, finally agreed in 1988. The other effect was to leave Britain in an isolated position as a major polluter still resisting international control. Britain was further isolated by the formation in 1984 of the '30% Club', a group of nations pledging themselves to a 30% reduction in sulphur dioxide emissions by 1993 (with 1980 as the base year). Britain declined to join, other notable absentees being the United States and Poland, both major sulphur dioxide producers. The only action conceded by the UK until 1986 was a research programme, to be conducted jointly by the CEGB and the National Coal Board over a period of five years. Many saw this as a cynical tactic designed to delay installation of pollution controls until the 1990s, when the CEGB hoped to be replacing coal-fired power stations with new nuclear capacity. However, in 1986, the position changed again.

In mid-1986 the apparent impasse was broken, when the British government gave the go-ahead to the CEGB to retrofit 6,000 MW of electricity generating plant (three large power stations) with flue gas desulphurisation equipment. A number of factors seemed to be behind this change of heart. First, new scientific evidence that a sulphur reservoir had built up in Scandinavian soils (and could only leach away if deposition declined) had influenced the CEGB and through them the government; second, a report from the influential House of Lords Committee dealing with European Community legislation had recommended that in spite of uncertainty about cause and effect, 'not less than two' power stations be fitted with FGD.[6] Finally, there was continuing political pressure for action from environmentalists, from the European Community and from Scandinavian countries; the FGD decision was announced immediately prior to a visit by the British Prime Minister to Norway. At this stage the British government was still firmly opposed to draft European Community legislation which was seeking a 60% reduction in sulphur dioxide emissions from large combustion plant by 1996 (using 1980 as the base year) and strict limits for sulphur dioxide, nitrogen oxides and particulates for new plant. This would have required a much bigger FGD retrofitting programme involving up to twelve British power stations.

The Large Combustion Plant Directive is an excellent example of the tortuous nature of international environmental policy-making (see Chapter 7). The UK opposed the draft Directive on grounds of cost and uncertainty, and poorer member states like Spain, Portugal and Eire, hoping for substantial economic growth and development, objected on the grounds of its implications for their power station construction programmes. After nearly five years of negotiation and redrafting the end result was inevitably a compromise. The form in which the Directive was finally agreed upon by Environment Ministers in 1988 is a 'watered down' version of the original. It allows for reduction of sulphur dioxide emissions to be made in three stages, and for the 60% reduction to be achieved by the year 2003, rather than 1995. Nitrogen oxide emissions are to be reduced by 30% by 1998, instead of by 40% by 1995 as originally proposed. Poorer member states were granted significant concessions; for example, Spain, which burns indigenous high-sulphur fuels, will be allowed (until the end of the century) to authorise new power stations that do not comply in full with sulphur dioxide emission limits in the Directive. It is unlikely that even this agreement could have been reached had not the British government made concessions because it was anxious to minimise uncertainty about emission controls expenditure in the run-up to electricity privatisation.

Equally tortuous has been the series of agreements on emissions from vehicle exhausts. Environment Ministers agreed in 1985 on a package of measures to reduce vehicle emissions (the 'Luxembourg Agreement') but it has been extremely difficult to achieve consensus because concern for the health of the environment is at least matched by the concern of some member states for the health of their motor industries. The 'small car' producers (UK, France, Italy and Spain) have consistently opposed stringent US-style controls, fearing that this would lead to a large increase in Japanese imports. 'Large vehicle' producers have allied with member states without car industries to press for stringent controls and a tighter timetable. The debate has been complex and difficult. Agreements on emission limits have now been reached which will require all new cars in the Community to be fitted with 'three-way catalytic converters' by the early 1990s, though the UK has always favoured 'lean-burn engines' for small cars, which would be cheaper and would reduce fuel consumption – but could not meet the stricter timetable which has ultimately been imposed. The agreement on small cars was reached in 1989 under new procedures arising from the Single European Act which give the European Parliament greater powers: increasingly conscious of the 'green vote' in Europe, MEPs voted for the first time to overturn a previous agreement on environmental policy in the Council of Environment Ministers. The European Commission then issued a revised proposal taking account of Parliament's wishes for more stringent controls, and this proposal was subsequently adopted (by majority voting) in the Council of Ministers.

Whether there is enough proof to justify action to reduce acid emissions is clearly less a scientific question than a political one. Genuine scientific uncertainty has permitted the protagonists in the acid rain debate to interpret each new set of research results in ways that support their own positions. Developing an environmental policy to cope with a major problem of this kind is a slow and difficult process, and the result is always a compromise. European legislation, for example, has been resisted by member states who perceive it as acting against their economic interests, yet others still consider what has been achieved to be too little too late. In the end, it is a question of politics; of whether the 'victims', or internal environmental consciousness, can exert sufficient political pressure on the polluters to force a change in attitude. Research will – and must – continue, but it is politics rather than science that is likely to determine the way in which this issue unfolds.

5   Non-renewable resources: the case of coal in Britain

Coal is a non-renewable mineral resource which has been of immense significance in the development of the British economy. In Chapter 3, some of the general principles of non-renewable resource estimation and depletion were introduced; in this chapter we consider the applicability of these principles in the real world, where perfect markets do not exist and decisions about resource exploitation impinge on the lives of real people. First we look at the extent of national coal reserves, then consider the factors that have influenced the level and location of coal production in Britain since the end of the Second World War. We then consider three fundamental issues that will affect the future shape of the coal industry: the economic efficiency of production; the social implications of improving efficiency in an industry with a strong regional base; and the environmental impacts of the coal fuel cycle, especially those associated with extraction and combustion.

British coal resources and reserves

Britain is richly endowed with coal and it is widely accepted that physical availability is unlikely to be a constraint on the development of this resource for the foreseeable future. But defining reserves is a different matter. The much-quoted figure of around 300 years' supply at current rates of production is based on the industry's own estimate of 'technically recoverable reserves' (roughly equivalent to 'proven reserves' in Fig. 3.6, Chapter 3), and it is interesting to see how it is derived. Total resources are very large, but much of the coal identified by geologists will not be of practical use because the effort involved in finding and recovering it would be too great; in other words, it does not fall into the category of 'reserves'. Potentially extractable coal is currently defined as that part of the resource base in deposits less than 1.2 kilometres deep, in seams thicker than 60 centimetres and having an ash content of no more than 20%. The total amount of such coal is estimated to be about 190 billion tonnes. About half of it (99 billion tonnes) is in known coalfields and the rest falls into the 'hypothetical' or 'speculative' categories. About 45% of the 99 billion tonnes is considered to be recoverable and marketable under current conditions. This is where the figure of 45 billion tonnes – or '300 years' supply' – comes from. In view of the uncertainty surrounding it, it is clearly not a very meaningful figure, and some critics have claimed that it is misleading. A much lower estimate of about fifty years' supply of coal was quoted by the Central Electricity Generating Board (CEGB), when defending its proposal for a new nuclear power station at Sizewell in Suffolk, demonstrating the essentially subjective nature of reserves estimates. For planning purposes the British Coal Corporation uses a much lower figure based on the concept of 'operating reserves' (around 4 billion tonnes in the mid-1980s), derived from local assessment at each mine and taking account of the availability of capital for investment. These are the reserves about which immediate investment decisions are made.

Uncertainty is unavoidable because the costs of exploration are high, and because accurate knowledge of reserves for long periods ahead is not necessary for the industry's internal planning. Exploration proceeds in stages, from 'potential prospects' – areas in which coal is believed to exist – through to actual development (the stage reached by the late 1980s at Asfordby mine in the Vale of Belvoir, Leicestershire), with more intensive survey work being involved at each stage (Fig. 5.1).

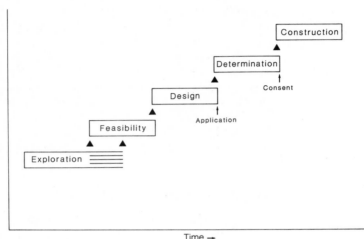

Fig. 5.1 Stages of exploration for coal. Exploration proceeds through various stages up to construction. Areas at different stages during the period 1973–85 are shown on the map below.

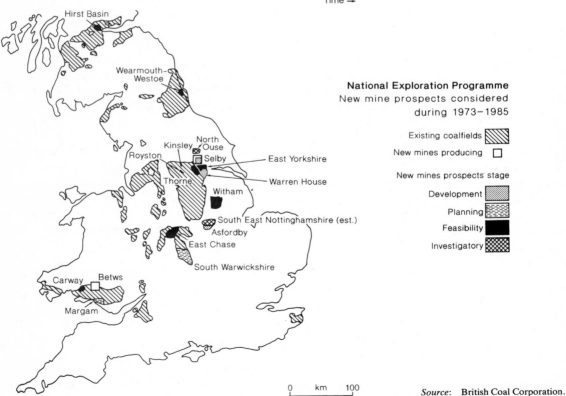

National Exploration Programme
New mine prospects considered during 1973–1985

Source: British Coal Corporation.

56

Geological data, seismic investigations and boreholes, from above and below ground, all provide information. Deep boreholes from the surface are very costly and require planning consents, so must themselves be regarded as a 'scarce resource'.

The pace of exploration – and therefore the rate of addition to reserves – responds dynamically to external circumstances. In the aftermath of the 1973 oil crisis, the rate of drilling, reaching 200 boreholes per year in 1977, was ten times the yearly average for the 1960s (when the industry was in decline), workable reserves were being increased at the rate of 500 million tonnes per year, and large economic deposits, as in the Vale of Belvoir, were proved. This was a classic response of the level of exploration activity and discovery to anticipated increases in demand and prices (see Fig. 3.7, Chapter 3).

With so much uncertainty, figures for UK coal reserves must be subject to continuous adjustment – most frequently for 'operating reserves', which change from year to year, and over longer periods for economically recoverable reserves as technology, prices and other conditions change. Given the physical abundance of coal in Britain, accurate estimates of total recoverable reserves are not what really matter. The important question is whether Britain's extensive reserves can be extracted at a cost that will permit coal to play a significant role in the country's energy future. Before considering the future, however, it is useful to look at the factors that have influenced the development of the British coal industry since the Second World War.

A brief post-war history

'King Coal' sustained the British economy throughout the Second World War, and at the time of nationalisation of the industry in 1947 was meeting about 90% of Britain's primary energy requirements. In the immediate post-war period output could not keep pace with rapidly growing energy demand. But since the mid-1950s, when post-war production peaked at 225 million tonnes, coal's contribution to the UK energy economy has declined steadily (Fig. 5.2). By 1988 it accounted

Fig. 5.2   Selected British coal industry statistics, 1947–1987/88.

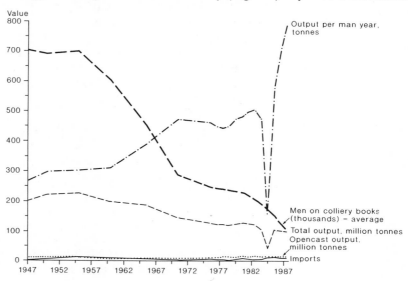

Source: **British Coal Corporation**, *Annual Report and Accounts*, 1987/88.

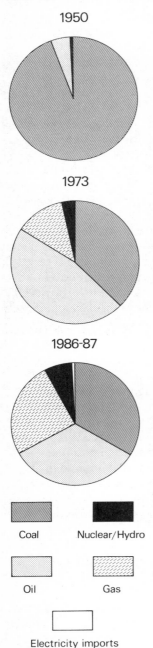

Fig. 5.3 Primary energy consumption in the UK, 1950–87.

1950

1973

1986-87

Coal

Nuclear/Hydro

Oil

Gas

Electricity imports

for only 35% of primary energy demand (Fig. 5.3). The pattern of use has also greatly changed, with some markets (e.g. for steam trains and town gas) disappearing altogether. The proportion of the industry's output consumed in power stations has increased very significantly, making the coal industry highly dependent on the electricity supply industry as its major customer. Since imports have been restricted (see below), there has effectively been a monopoly, and with one dominant customer it is clear that the situation has been very far removed from the perfect market envisaged in theoretical models of resource depletion.

One major factor in coal's decline was increased competition from oil and gas, initially imported but from the early 1970s supplied in increasing quantities from the North Sea. *Resource substitution* took place over two decades in many markets as cheaper, cleaner and more convenient fuels became available; this process cannot easily be reversed when prices change. Other factors behind the decline were increased nuclear power capacity, adoption of smokeless zones (designated in the 1956 Clean Air Act) and improvements in fuel efficiency. All of these factors meant that the proportion of the resource base that could be produced economically diminished. According to the theory outlined in Chapter 3, we would expect coal to be mined if the rate of return from investing the profits exceeds the rate of appreciation of the value of the coal in the ground. However, intervention (by governments of all persuasions) to mitigate the social effects of decline has meant that significant amounts of coal have been produced at costs well above the price for which the product can be sold. 'Economic efficiency', as defined in Chapter 3, has not been achieved.

After the dramatic fourfold increase in the price of oil in 1973/74, coal regained a price advantage and the strategic benefits of indigenous resources were rediscovered. Ambitious plans to revive the industry were hastily drawn up. A new *Plan for Coal* announced by the Labour Government in 1974 envisaged an increase in production from around 120 million tonnes per annum to 170 million tonnes per annum by the year 2000, to be achieved by new investment in existing mines and by the opening up of new capacity, much of it in greenfield sites. Exploration was stepped up and the scene was set for significant expansion of the industry. The 'scarcity' which induced this classic response was not, however, the result of unfettered operation of world market forces, but was caused by the Organisation of Petroleum Exporting Countries (OPEC) exercising its oligopolistic powers to keep oil in the ground!

But the bright hopes embodied in *Plan for Coal* were never realised. Deep economic recession followed the oil crisis and growth in total energy demand was much lower than expected (a very good example of the inherent uncertainty in forecasting). As the decade progressed, coal's price advantage was eroded as oil prices fell again in real terms and the availability of North Sea gas increased. Whereas *Plan for Coal* had envisaged expanding markets, especially in industry, in fact in the period 1970–85 demand outside the power station market fell by 60%. The National Coal Board (renamed the British Coal Corporation in 1987) lapsed heavily into deficit from 1980 onwards, and was soon placed under intense pressure by the strongly 'pro-market'

Sheffield miners lobby an executive meeting during the 1984 miners' strike.

Conservative Government elected in 1979. The Coal Industry Act of 1980 stipulated that the National Coal Board should break even by 1985, which meant closing the 'tail' of high-cost pits. In response to these plans the National Union of Mineworkers (NUM) imposed an overtime ban from 31st October 1983. Soon afterwards a decision to bring forward the closure of Cortonwood Colliery in Scotland precipitated the divisive miners' strike which began in March 1984 and ended with defeat for the miners and their return to work a year later.

Although the 'break-even' target was eventually put back to 1988/89, political and economic pressures on the coal industry intensified during the 1980s. With a government ideologically opposed to intervention, falling world market prices and the prospect of a privatised electricity industry free to buy imported coal, a painful process of readjustment towards 'economic efficiency' has taken place. The British Coal Corporation embarked on a major programme of restructuring and introduced a new management strategy which effectively relegates from the category of 'proven reserves' any deposits that cannot be mined in accordance with strict financial criteria set to reflect anticipated world market conditions. This new strategy has accelerated the closure of uneconomic pits (as defined by the Corporation's financial targets) and the concentration of production into modern, high-productivity mines. Less coal will be extracted from the older, peripheral coalfields and more from central areas. Overall, the effect may well be that under the new regime less coal will be extracted in Britain now because it is more 'efficient' to extract this resource elsewhere (or in the future). However, the question of imported coal is politically a very sensitive one, and it is worth considering in rather more detail.

New technology, including computerised systems for remote control and monitoring of colliery activities, means that mines can now operate with a much smaller workforce than was previously required. In the early 1990s, for example, this new mine at Selby is expected to be producing 12.5 million tonnes of coal per annum with some 3,500–4,000 miners. In contrast, in the mid-1980s, combined production from the South Wales and Scottish coalfields, employing some 39,000 miners, was about 13.5 million tonnes.

British coal and the world market

In an open market, the fortunes of a resource-based industry in any one country will depend on its ability to compete with foreign suppliers (or with substitutes). However, governments frequently protect indigenous industries, through import barriers or subsidies, on grounds of security of supply, balance of payments or social or regional policy. All British governments have afforded protection to the coal industry in this way, but the Thatcher administration was markedly less ready to intervene than any of its predecessors.

The price of coal on the world market fell in the second half of the 1980s and many analysts feel that it is unlikely to rise very much in real terms for some time to come. The House of Commons Select Committee on Energy (the Energy Committee) identified the following reasons for this state of affairs.[1]

- very low production costs of some suppliers, due to favourable geology, ease of extraction (often by surface mining) and efficient mining operations;
- supply expansion in the 1970s in classic response to the oil crisis, resulting in surplus capacity when demand failed to grow on anything like the scale expected (demonstrating that producers have far from perfect knowledge of the future);
- willingness of some producers to sell at prices that barely cover their costs (some have been accused of 'dumping' – selling on foreign markets at prices below marginal production costs);
- low transport costs to port of export, and internationally, because of a depressed ocean freight market;
- absence of any dominant cartel (like OPEC) in the world coal market (i.e. no monopolistic or oligopolistic pressure to reduce the rate of extraction of this resource).

Table 5.1 Internationally traded steam coal

Country of origin	Total delivered cost (ARA),[1] £/tonne	Spot prices c.i.f. Europe,[2] £/tonne
South Africa		
Opencast	14.00	
Underground	17.66	18.33
Richards Bay Phase IV opencast	19.00	
Australia		
Queensland new opencast	22.88	
New South Wales opencast	28.55	21.33
New South Wales underground	28.88	
Colombia		
New opencast	37.30	22.70–24.00
USA		
Large opencast	31.00	25.70

[1] ARA – delivery to Amsterdam/Rotterdam/Antwerp
[2] c.i.f. Europe – spot price in Europe including cost, insurance and freight

Source: **House of Commons Select Committee on Energy** (1987) *The Coal Industry*, First Report, Session 1986–87, HMSO, London.

Producers in Australia, Canada, Colombia, South Africa and the United States of America have been able to deliver coal to Western Europe at prices below UK production costs (£42 per tonne on average, 1988) and are likely to continue to supply low-price coal for the foreseeable future (Table 5.1). The situation may not be stable in the longer term; world production and transport facilities should eventually come into balance with demand, and if the sterling/dollar exchange rate moved in favour of the dollar, imports would become less competitive in the UK. But the Energy Committee summed up the situation in 1987 as one in which

> . . . there is ample existing and potential low-cost mining capacity available in the rest of the world to pose a challenge to the British industry.

The traditionally low level of coal imports to the UK has resulted in part from deliberate policies, including a ban on imports in the 1960s, which have encouraged or coerced British consumers into buying home-produced coal, and in part from the protection afforded by lack of infrastructure and locational factors. Facilities to handle large coal carriers at British ports are limited and many customers (for example the majority of coal-fired power stations) lie inland, so are further protected by high overland transport costs. Coal costing £27 per tonne on the Rotterdam 'spot' market in 1985 would have cost a further £4.70 per tonne (after trans-shipment) to reach lower Thameside, and a further £14.75 per tonne to be delivered to Didcot power station in Oxfordshire via a Bristol Channel port. These circumstances are not immutable, however, because capital investment could be committed to port facilities, and the location of future coal-using plant is flexible. There is little doubt that the British Coal Corporation's major customers would like to be free to buy coal on the world market if prices were attractive. Imports rose during the miners' strike and have been maintained at a relatively high level since then. The British Steel Corporation doubled its imports between 1980/81 and 1985/86, and the Central Electricity Generating Board (CEGB), its bargaining position strengthened by falling world fossil fuel prices, was able to negotiate a new 'joint understanding' with British Coal, to run until March 1991, under which an increasing proportion of the CEGB's purchases from the British Coal Corporation are aligned with the price of imported coal and oil. A privatised electricity industry is likely to be even more anxious to minimise the cost of its raw materials. Highly polarised views are held on the subject of coal imports and as usual in such circumstances, inherent uncertainty is manipulated to suit the arguments of the various protagonists. Some free-marketeers urge that the UK should import as much coal as is available at prices below British production costs. They argue that this would stimulate greater efficiency in coal production, leading to lower prices and to benefits for industry, other consumers and the economy as a whole. It is even suggested that in the longer term, coal's market share might expand as it became more competitive with other fuels. Those taking a protectionist stance (including the miners' unions) maintain that some producers achieve low prices by exploiting labour and/or the environment, or by 'dumping'. (In other words, the world 'market' is itself highly imperfect.) They warn that imports would make the British economy vulnerable to future disruption and that the import bill would be detrimental to the balance of payments. The validity of all of these points can be debated at length (see 'Further reading'). What is undeniable is that imports would, at least in the short term, displace domestic production and hence jobs. Some observers consider that the social cost of this displacement – even if only readily quantifiable costs are counted – would outweigh any savings in the economy as a whole. The Energy Committee took the view that the *option* of imports should be kept open to act as a competitive spur to the British Coal Corporation, but also urged vigilance against unfair competition. Without protection, however, the industry would need to respond to the threat of imports just as it would respond to the reality – by reducing costs and increasing productivity (that is, increasing 'technological efficiency') in order to become competitive in a wider market. This is what happened in the years following the miners' strike: by 1988 the workforce had been almost halved (from 221,000 to 117,000), 78 pits had been closed or merged and productivity (output per man year) had increased by around 60%.

The Energy Committee, in its 1987 Report, acknowledged the 'remarkable and commendable progress' made by the industry but also noted that it had been achieved at very high cost to the taxpayer and mining communities. It is to the question of these costs that we now turn.

Social costs

We have seen that not all production of coal in Britain since the Second World War has been economically 'efficient' in the strict sense, but the industry has been protected from full exposure to market forces by

'Pentre Diwaith' – village without work. The social impacts of decline of a major industry can be severe.

successive governments for social and strategic reasons. A major change in the political climate in the 1980s has forced the industry into restructuring and, as is always the case when new policies affect the way in which resources are exploited, some people gain and others lose in the process. As we have seen in Chapter 3, analysis of costs and benefits in the aggregate (as in the neo-classical models) can be fairly meaningless; social and spatial distribution matters, and it is clear that different policies towards the development of coal resources have very different distributive consequences. This is what makes the issue so contentious.

In the case of pit closure, for example, some costs, such as care and maintenance of the mine after closure, are borne directly by the British Coal Corporation. Redundancy payments, loss of tax revenue and the cost of unemployment benefits are borne by the government (that is, the taxpayer). But the wider, less easily quantifiable social costs of unemployment and economic decay fall heavily on mining areas, which, as the Energy Committee points out, have characteristics which make them particularly vulnerable. They tend to be

> dominated by a single industry and . . . divided into large numbers of dispersed relatively small communities, geographically isolated and heavily self-dependent. These communities have few

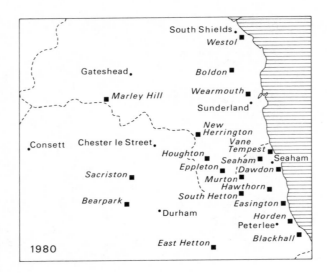

Fig. 5.4   Pits in County Durham, 1980–87.

non-mining infrastructural amenities, and a social and cultural tradition which is both distinctive and mining related. These features act as a disincentive to the inward investment necessary to replace jobs in mining.[1]

The scale of pit closures in any one area can be drastic, as indicated by the maps in Fig. 5.4.

In any wider assessment of costs and benefits, the detrimental effects of retaining high-cost pits has to be considered too. These include high energy costs for other industries (possibly leading to job losses), government subsidies (which must ultimately be paid by someone), and the monopoly-enhancing effects of protectionism. Where should the line be drawn in deciding whether a pit is 'economic'?

The leader of the National Union of Mineworkers, Arther Scargill, has often argued that it costs more money to close a pit than it does to keep it open, but others maintain that wider costs have to be ignored for decision purposes, because, as one analyst argues:

> Even if in the short term they exceed the saving from closure, in the long term their retention will once again shackle the NCB with an inheritance of unmanageable and uneconomic assets.[2]

The social cost-benefit analysis is clearly very complex and some people believe that a nationalised industry should take a wider view of its responsibilities than a private company. But the Energy Committee, while agreeing that British Coal has a responsibility to mitigate the short-term economic and environmental effects of closure (and to give adequate warning), argues that the wider responsibility falls elsewhere:

> If the macro-economic and social disbenefits of the policies of the management of a strategic industry like coal outweigh the benefits to society of those policies, then it is the job of government to right the balance by fiscal or other means.[1]

Where exactly that balance is struck depends on the ideology of the government in power and its susceptibility to pressure from the various interest groups involved.

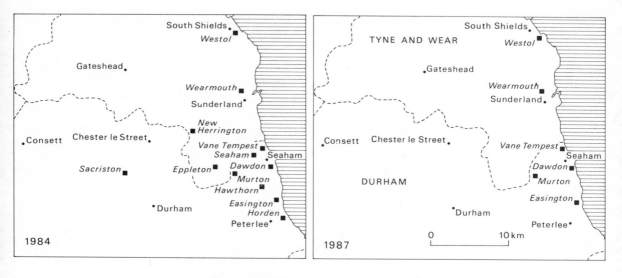

Source: **Benyon, H.** (1987) 'Nationalisation and planning in the regions: critical questions from the North of England', presented at a conference on *Coal on the Energy Seesaw*, Nottingham, April 1987, sponsored by the UK Centre for Economic and Environmental Development, London.

Mitigating the effects of decline

Successive governments have attempted to mitigate the social impact of job losses in coal mining directly with grants and subsidies and indirectly through regional policy, job creation programmes and other schemes. In 1984 the then National Coal Board established British Coal Enterprise Ltd (BCE) to help create long-term employment opportunities in traditional coalmining areas. By 1988 BCE, with access to funding from the Department of Energy, had committed £43 million to help create some 29,000 jobs. But against a background of 'de-industrialisation' and high unemployment in traditional mining areas, the task is a difficult one. New towns, inner cities and other depressed regions compete for a diminishing number of jobs, and resources allocated to regional aid have been progressively reduced. Migration to find employment in more prosperous areas is inhibited by housing costs – and only exacerbates the problems of the community left behind. It is difficult to avoid the conclusion of the Energy Committee:

> Such is the scale and the likely persistence of unemployment in the mining communities that a radical reconsideration of the most effective response of Government is urgently required.[1]

The way forward, in the Committee's view, is to proceed with rationalisation of the coal industry but with much more substantial efforts to alleviate the social problems involved – 'not merely a higher level of resources, but a commitment of energy, imagination and purpose'. Others, doubting that such commitment could be summoned or channelled effectively, conclude that the only way to avoid 'writing off' whole communities is to preserve jobs in mining, at least in the short to medium term. To that end some observers have urged a moratorium on nuclear power, restriction of opencast production (discussed below) and a ban on imports of coal or electricity.[3] It seems

65

most unlikely, however, that such restrictions will be imposed, especially as the coal industry itself has been identified as a candidate for privatisation.

Inevitably, then, there are significant social implications when the rate and location of resource extraction is changed. There are also important environmental impacts, which will be considered below.

Environmental impacts

The exploitation of non-renewable resources inevitably impinges upon other resource functions. As we have seen in Chapter 1, environmental concern has focused increasingly on the impacts of resource extraction, like pollution or effects on amenity, rather than on depletion of a finite resource stock. The trend towards concern for the environment rather than concern about depletion is clearly apparent in the case of coal. In fact, the availability of coal for future generations has hardly been an issue at all, either in the heated debate about pit closures, or in the conflict over developing new mining capacity.

All stages of the coal fuel cycle involve significant environmental impact (Table 5.2). Here we focus on *extraction*, which involves land take, subsidence (after deep mining), visual intrusion and air, water and noise pollution, and *combustion*, a major contributor to urban air pollution in the past, and now implicated in both acid rain and the greenhouse effect.

In the past, the environmental costs of coal extraction were largely externalised by the industry, to be borne by generations of inhabitants of mining communities. Now environmental controls on all stages of the fuel cycle are much more stringent, and tight planning and pollution control conditions are imposed on all new developments. Impacts can

Table 5.2 Environmental impacts of the coal energy cycle

	Air	Water	Land	Wildlife	Others
Extraction, treatment, transport and waste disposal	Sulphur oxides, nitrogen oxides, particulates	Acid mine drainage Mine liquid waste disposal Water availability Wash water treatment Water pollution from storage heaps	Subsidence Land take Permanent loss of historical features	Habitat disturbance Wilderness exploitation	Noise Dust Visual impact Occupational risks
Electricity generation/ combustion	Sulphur oxides, nitrogen oxides, carbon monoxide, carbon dioxide, hydrocarbons, trace elements, particulates, radionuclides Transboundary pollution	Water availability Thermal releases	Land take	Secondary effects on water, air and land	Visual impact Solid wastes Noise

Source: **Organisation for Economic Co-operation and Development** (1985) *The State of the Environment*, OECD, Paris.

be mitigated by good design, control of air, water and noise pollution, measures to prevent subsidence, and progressive reclamation and rehabilitation of land affected by mining or waste disposal.

Considerable progress has been made in all of these areas, but the coal industry is still environmentally controversial; indeed many of the issues were subject to unprecedented scrutiny in the 1970s and 1980s, as the industry sought to expand its activities into greenfield sites with no previous history of mining, and as the profitable Opencast Executive (a semi-autonomous branch of the British Coal Corporation) has seemed determined to pursue expansionary production targets. Here we consider some of the more significant issues: the controversy over greenfield sites for new deep mines, conflict over opencast developments, and some of the environmental implications of coal combustion.

Greenfield sites

The then National Coal Board (NCB) faced its first-ever public inquiry into a new deep mine when it applied to develop the Selby coalfield in a predominantly rural part of North Yorkshire in 1976. There was considerable local anxiety about the potential impact of subsidence on drainage in the low-lying agricultural plain, and concern about the environmental and social impact of the new mine and all its associated facilities. But in the immediate aftermath of the oil crisis there seemed little doubt about the need to develop new coal reserves, and consent was granted subject to stringent conditions. These included limits on subsidence (0.99 metres) and the height of the shift headgear (30 metres), and a stipulation that pillars of coal be left to support Selby Abbey. Arrangements were made to keep all environmental impacts under review as the mine was developed and operated.

When, in 1978, the NCB applied to sink three mines in the Vale of Belvoir in north-east Leicestershire, resistance was more entrenched. Leicestershire County Council and other local authorities opposed the development and an alliance of agricultural, amenity and residents' groups (led by the Duke of Rutland, whose seat is Belvoir Castle) fought the proposal bitterly at a lengthy public inquiry. The main issue was the impact of mining and associated infrastructure on an unspoilt part of rural Britain. Spoil disposal became a major bone of contention; Belvoir coal (unlike that from Selby) would be relatively 'dirty'. Residents wanted spoil removed to disused clay pits in Bedfordshire, but neither the NCB nor the owners of the holes in the ground (the London Brick Company) were willing to contemplate the high transport costs. Perhaps the most interesting development was that by the time of the Belvoir inquiry in 1979/80, when energy demand forecasts were already being revised steeply downwards, the debate was not so much about 'national need versus local amenity' as about the *need* for the coal itself. Objectors engaged experts who vigorously challenged the NCB and government forecasts and argued that the 'need' for Belvoir coal was so questionable that despoilation of the Vale could not possibly be justified. It is interesting that in both Selby and Belvoir, objections were to the environmental impact of mining, rather than to depletion of coal reserves – a good example of the way in which environmental concerns have shifted since the late 1960s, as noted above. The British Coal Corporation has faced strong opposition to development of a new mine

at Hawkhurst Moor in the green belt of south Warwickshire, and has prepared a major environmental impact assessment for scrutiny at the public inquiry. It seems almost certain to face such opposition wherever it attempts to develop greenfield sites. The implications, given that many 'prospects' are in rural areas (see map, Fig. 5.1), are that the development of new, low-cost capacity will be accompanied by serious environmental conflict.

The opencast dilemma

British opencast coal mining began in 1942 as an emergency wartime measure. By the end of the 1960s, output had fallen to around 7 million tonnes per annum, but in the wake of the oil crisis a target of 15 million tonnes per annum was set and was achieved by the beginning of the 1980s. The Opencast Executive (OCE) is a distinctive part of the British Coal Corporation. It owns most of the country's opencast sites, but the actual mining is contracted out to civil engineering firms.

Although it accounts for a relatively small proportion of UK coal production, opencast mining is inherently an environmentally intrusive operation. Approximately 30 tonnes of 'overburden' (the rock lying above the coal seam) have to be removed for every tonne of coal produced. Extensive areas of land are involved. The Commission on Energy and the Environment (CENE) concluded in a major study of the coal industry that

> . . . even if the greatest care is taken in both extraction of opencast coal and the subsequent restoration of the land . . . opencast mining has a severe impact on the environment in both the long and short term,[4]

and the House of Commons Select Committee on Energy agreed that

> opencast mining is one of the most environmentally destructive processes being carried out in the UK.[1]

Rehabilitation and landscaping: this 'American Adventure Park' in Derbyshire was once a site of opencast coal extraction.

But opencast mining is profitable, and as financial pressures on the British Coal Corporation have intensified, it has sought to expand opencast production in the face of strong opposition from environmental interests. This is a classic environmental conflict, complicated by the wider problems being faced by the British coal industry. As well as the environmental impact, a major issue is the extent to which opencast production subsidises and supports, or is in straightforward competition with, production from less profitable deep mines.

The Opencast Executive argues that opencast production contributes to special market needs (e.g. anthracite and coking coal) and supports deep-mined production by reducing average costs in the industry and by providing coal which can 'sweeten' deep-mined coal with a high chlorine content, which would otherwise have to remain in the ground. Environmental groups maintain that the bulk of opencast production is not used for 'special' purposes but is burned in power stations, and have argued that the *marginal cost* of producing coal even from high-cost deep mines is less than that from new opencast sites, because the latter must include all the costs of development. The OCE points to its record on restoration; opponents argue that although land can be restored to agriculture and other uses, features like ancient hedgerows are irretrievably lost.

Many environmentalists (and local communities) believe that the environmental costs of opencast production are unacceptably high, that the benefits are exaggerated by the OCE, and that in the absence of an overriding national need for coal, opencast mining should be phased out. Even the government-appointed Commission on Energy and the Environment (CENE) recommended that opencast mining should be confined to areas where coal reserves were in danger of sterilisation by development, where it could form part of a programme to restore land or where there was a demonstrable need (for special coal or because of rapidly increasing demand). However, the balance seems to have tipped against the environmental argument during the 1980s. The government rejected CENE's recommendation that there should be a 15 million tonnes per annum ceiling on production, saying that the level of output should be determined by market forces, subject to the acceptability of individual projects as determined by the planning system. A 1987 draft circular to planning authorities from the Department of the Environment excluded all references to the 'need' for coal or to the restriction of opencast mining to environmentally acceptable sites, making it extremely difficult for local authorities to balance economic needs and environmental impacts. This is an excellent example of the fundamental issue raised in Chapter 2: how 'need' is defined, whether it should be equated with 'demand', and whether it should be met in the face of significant, but not easily quantifiable, environmental costs. In 1986 the OCE outraged its opposition by seeking to *increase* production to 18 million tonnes per annum, and possibly beyond, implying a 25% increase in land take which already (at 2,000–4,000 hectares per annum) means that on average a new site has to be opened every three weeks. Conflict is likely to intensify as the OCE increasingly seeks to develop greenfield sites, which cannot offer the significant compensation of removal of existing dereliction.

Coal combustion

Some of the most significant environmental impacts of coal combustion are considered in Chapter 4 where we discuss the problem of acid rain and possible solutions to it. Acid emissions and particulates from coal combustion can be controlled by known technologies even if, as shown in Chapter 4, such control is expensive. A more intractable problem is that of the production of carbon dioxide (CO_2), which is an unavoidable result of the combustion of fossil fuels since this involves the oxidation of carbon. A modern coal-fired power station, for example, burning 5 million tonnes of coal each year, would produce around 11 million tonnes of carbon dioxide. Carbon dioxide is naturally present in the atmosphere, but its concentration is rising and since it is a 'greenhouse gas'[5], there are fears that increasing concentrations will lead to global warming, sea-level rise and climatic change, with potentially disastrous consequences in many parts of the world. There are other greenhouse gases (for example methane, and the chlorofluorocarbons (CFCs)), but experts consider that CO_2 is responsible for about 50% of the greenhouse effect, with CO_2 emissions from coal-fired power stations accounting for about 10%.

The only practicable way to reduce CO_2 emissions from coal combustion is to burn less coal. Whereas sulphur and nitrogen oxides can be removed by flue gas scrubbing (see Chapter 4), no equivalent technology exists to remove CO_2. New technologies may, however, enable us to burn coal much more efficiently, as well as minimising emissions of sulphur and nitrogen oxides. One technology now at an advanced stage is fluidised bed combustion (FBC), in which coal in a 'bed' of fine inert particles like sand or ash, is 'fluidised' by a stream of air entering the bottom of the combuster. The British Coal Corporation has an experimental pressurised FBC unit at Grimethorpe in South Yorkshire. Another promising possibility is the 'integrated gasification combined cycle' in which coal is gasified and the gas burned in a gas turbine, from which the hot exhaust gases are fed to waste heat boilers which raise steam for a steam turbine. A demonstration system has been operating at Cool Water, California, since 1984 and is the world's cleanest coal-fired power station.

These technologies convert coal to electricity with efficiencies of over 40%, which may be improved further as they develop, compared with a maximum for conventional power stations of 38.5%. Although they do not remove CO_2, they obviously produce less of it for a given energy output than conventional systems, and they do reduce other emissions. But they are not without problems: both technologies have a large limestone consumption, generate significant amounts of waste, and still require further technological development before they become commercially available on a large scale.

Clearly, the coal fuel cycle will never be without environmental impacts. But whereas the environmental costs of the cycle used to be largely 'externalised' (see Chapter 3), they are now increasingly internalised in that the coal industry and users of coal have to bear the cost of minimising environmental degradation and pollution. Thus the costs of producing and using coal better (though still imperfectly) reflect the true social costs of exploiting this resource. State intervention to ensure that environmental costs are internalised (for example in pollution control or land use planning legislation) will mean that less coal is produced than would otherwise be the case.

Concluding comments

This chapter has shown that the level of coal production in Britain has responded in very general terms to changes in market conditions; less coal has been produced as cheaper and more convenient substitutes have become available. But the amount of the resource extracted, especially in the older, peripheral coalfields, has been greater than it would have been under the free market conditions since every government – even the most non-interventionist – has subsidised and protected the industry to some extent. Two factors have justified such policies: the strategic advantages of an indigenous resource, and the unacceptable social consequences of the uncontrolled decline of a geographically concentrated industry. As the industry has been increasingly exposed to the world market (which is itself imperfect) it has been forced to restructure and to close high-cost capacity, with significant social implications. Less coal might also have been extracted if the full environmental costs of the coal fuel cycle had been internalised; pressure for internalisation of costs has grown and is likely to increase further in future.

What we can say is that there is inherent uncertainty about coal reserves, that the rate of depletion is determined by many non-market factors, and that the full social costs of production are rarely reflected in the price. In seeking to understand the exploitation of non-renewable resources, it is crucial to take all such issues into account, for market imperfections are likely to continue to be the dominant factors influencing the use of resources in the real world.

6 Renewable resource management: the Norfolk Broads

Britain's countryside has been undergoing rapid change, which has brought the interests of conservation, agriculture and recreation into conflict with each other. Nowhere better illustrates the complexity of this triangular relationship, or the difficulty of managing multipurpose renewable resources, than the Norfolk Broads, a wetland of fens and marshes in north-east Suffolk and Norfolk (Fig. 6.1). In at least three

Fig. 6.1 The Norfolk Broads.

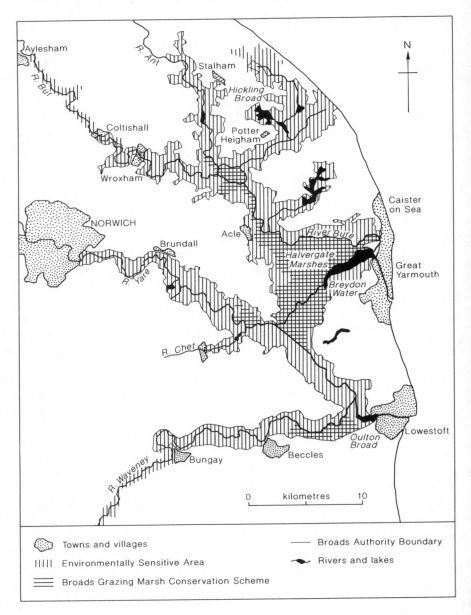

Sailing on Hickling Broad.

instances – the serious and apparently unarrested decline of the waterways, the unconstrained agricultural intensification affecting Halvergate Marshes, and pressures from explosive growth of tourism and recreation – conservationists' sense of outrage has given rise to nationally important controversies. The common factor in all of this was poor resource management. The purpose of this chapter is to explain why the Broads are important and precious and to use the controversies that have arisen as a practical illustration of the complexity of issues involved.

Origin and natural history

Broadland is associated with three principal rivers, the Yare, Bure and Waveney, which flow rather sluggishly, for most of the area is less than 30 metres above sea-level. The broads themselves – and there are more than forty of them – are shallow lakes. Hickling Broad, the largest at 122 hectares, is a great sheet of water, but many broads are small and only a few centimetres deep. On first acquaintance the landscape can appear flat and monotonous, but the wonder of Broadland lies in its great variety of ecology and land use, and the multitude of natural and semi-natural habitats developed down the centuries through symbiosis of natural environmental processes and human interference in the form of a traditional marshland economy. There is access to all these diverse environments from an uninterrupted navigation of 210 km, and as a result the ecological importance of the Broads is internationally recognised.

The Broads originated from a combination of natural and human influences that produced a regular succession of vegetation change, the relict stages of which can still be seen today (Fig. 6.2). The broads are not natural lakes, but are the stepped and steep-sided remnants of *turbaries* (peat pits), first begun by the Danes around AD 800–900 to

Aerial views of Broadland show the great variety of land use.

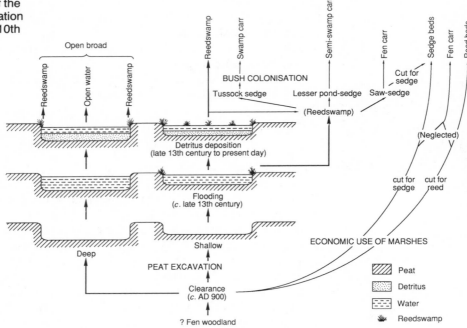

Fig. 6.2 Origin of the Broads and vegetation change since the 10th century.

Open broad

Reedswamp | Open water | Reedswamp

Reedswamp

Swamp carr

Semi-swamp carr

Fen carr

Sedge beds

Fen carr

Reed beds

BUSH COLONISATION

Cut for sedge

Tussock sedge   Lesser pond-sedge   Saw-sedge

(Reedswamp)

(Neglected)

Detritus deposition
(late 13th century to present day)

Flooding
(c. late 13th century)

cut for sedge   cut for reed

Shallow

ECONOMIC USE OF MARSHES

Deep

PEAT EXCAVATION

Clearance
(c. AD 900)

? Fen woodland

Peat

Detritus

Water

Reedswamp

Source: **Nature Conservancy Council** (1965) *Report on Broadland*, p.15.

tap a local source of fuel. The diggings became flooded in the 14th century and have shown a natural tendency to infill ever since. Once the depth of a broad reduces to a critical level – about one metre – vegetation begins to replace open water. Reedswamp becomes established, and is succeeded by sedges; later, alder woodland replaces the open fen.

The Broads have long served an economic purpose, supplying renewable resources such as peat, reed, sedge, marsh litter and alder poles. The waterways, although primarily a resource for tourism and recreation today, were historically important as a commercial fishery and navigation system. Whenever there has been one or more of these

Reeds are harvested at How Hill on the river Ant for use in traditional thatching.

forms of resource management the natural succession has been arrested, so helping to sustain and diversify the environment. The landscapes that reflect these aspects of the marshland economy are most characteristic of the upper reaches of the Broadland rivers, where the peat is thick. Nearer the sea there is only a thin layer of peat over clay, and from about 1800, enclosure provided an incentive for landowners to introduce drainage and convert the fen to grazing marsh. Gradually the land shrank and sank and a new patchwork landscape of river embankments and drainage ditches, relieved by a scatter of windmills, was created.

Decline of the Broads

Over the centuries the Broads became an unrivalled example of environmental enhancement through sustainable husbandry. The idyll so evocatively captured by 19th-century photographers[1] shows us a marshland of clear waters and a wide variety of water plants. Now this enchanting scene has given way to a depleted environment of phytoplankton-laden 'pea soup' from which water plants have more or less completely disappeared. Although traditional cropping practices were gradually abandoned from the latter part of the 19th century, and much open water was replaced by alder woodland and grazing marshes, a new phase of rapid and serious decline began around 1950 (Fig. 6.3).

Fig. 6.3   Links between Broadland's problems.

Source: **Moss, B.** (1987) 'The Broads', *Biologist* **34**, p.10.

The transition is bound up with changes in water chemistry. It was the naturally alkaline water of the rivers and broads, draining from a fertile catchment, that nurtured the wide variety of flora and fauna, but recent changes in the balance of certain nutrients have undermined the

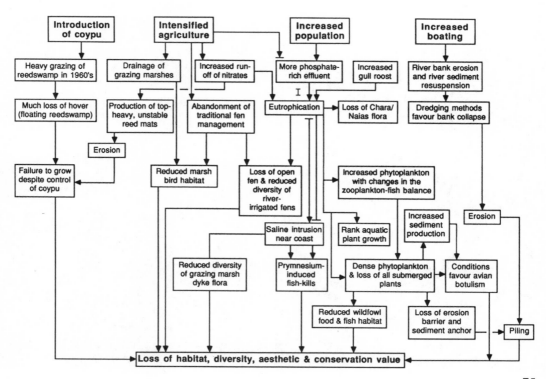

75

Fig. 6.4 Three stages in
the decline of the Norfolk
Broads.

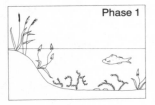

Phase 1

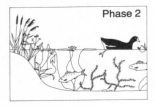

Phase 2

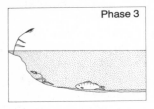

Phase 3

Source: Adapted from
The Broads Authority (1987)
Broads Plan, p.19.

ecosystem. For example, phosphorus is particularly important because it acts as a limiting factor on plant growth, and for various reasons it is now much more abundant in the Broads. These environmental changes are being investigated in an important research programme led by the ecologist, Brian Moss.[2]

Until well into the 19th century the Broads were clean and clear, and a *low plant community* (phase 1, Fig. 6.4) was characteristic. Phosphorus loadings of 20 micrograms per litre were typical and nitrogen levels were about twenty times greater. Algae were sparse, light penetrated several metres of water, and the relatively low nutrient levels supported a diverse flora and fauna, notably a dense sward of low-growing charophytes (stoneworts) on the bottom.

Tall plant communities (phase 2, Fig. 6.4) became important and succeeded until about 1950. Then phosphorus levels increased to about 50 micrograms per litre, as Norfolk's towns and villages were gradually connected to mains sewerage and effluents began to be discharged into the rivers. Nitrogen levels also increased, mainly because of physical disturbance caused by a more mechanised agriculture, and the new nutrient levels supported more algal and plant growth. Strongly growing tall plants such as fennel-leaved pondweed (*Potamogeton pectinatus*), spiked water milfoil (*Myriophyllum spicatum*), hornwort (*Ceratophyllum demersum*) and water soldier (*Stratiotes aloides*) flourished. These plants enjoyed the greater nutrient supply and could compete well for light in the more algal water. This fertile phase also supported an abundant fauna including enhanced fish populations, and the river banks were well protected by reeds and the further buffer of tall plants. It is this tall plant phase that has come to epitomise our image of the Broads.

a

(a) Plant-depleted waters and bank erosion on the river Bure. (b) An adjacent plant-filled dyke on the Bure.

b

Today, a *heavy algal growth phase* is typical (phase 3, Fig. 6.4). It represents a serious loss of habitat and threatens the survival of this otherwise renewable resource. Waters with a tall plant community are high in nitrogen, but phosphorus continues to be a limiting factor. Since the mid-1940s, nitrogen supply has been boosted again, this time because of heavy use of artificial fertilizers that wash off surrounding farmland, and phosphorus has become abundant (typically 200–300 micrograms per litre). It reaches the rivers in sewage effluent loaded with the phosphate-rich detergents that became widely available after 1950. Thus the Broads became a sink for pollution and went into decline. Because of *eutrophication* (nutrient enrichment), phytoplankton multiplies, shades out young plant shoots and rapidly transforms the habitat into a barren 'pea soup'. Aquatic plants are more or less absent and the effect on fish populations is significant; the lost plants no longer provide a habitat for the fauna – mainly water fleas – on which fish feed. Effects of boat traffic are also exacerbated since plant removal makes first bankside reeds and then the bank itself more vulnerable to wash erosion. Infill of the broads has reached 1%–2% per year, which is serious because overall depths of only a metre are not uncommon.

This three-phase model is oversimplified, but the degradation is clear and underlies the urgent need for resource management in the interests of both conservation and recreation. Since eutrophication is seen as the key factor, restorative measures have been concentrated on attempts to restrict nutrient supply, in particular the input of phosphorus, because nitrate, being readily soluble in water and derived from a multiplicity of sources, is much harder to control. Alderfen Broad became a test site when in the winter of 1978 effluent was diverted away from the broad by isolating it from the main river channel. The following summer algae bloomed as before, but in 1980/81 phosphorus release halved, taking down the level of phytoplankton, and in 1982 net release of phosphorus ceased. The water cleared and plants spread over the floor of the broad. By 1983 there was a phase 2 community and the experiment seemed a success. But in 1984 and 1985 the plants died back; isolation had also eliminated flushing, and the new plants quickly de-oxygenated the bottom sediment, causing phosphate release and a reassertion of phytoplankton. A second site, Cockshoot Broad, was isolated in 1982. This time the sediment was mechanically pumped out of the broad, and plants re-established more successfully. This success is encouraging, but of limited appeal because the cost of pumping is prohibitive, and navigation rights – which add a common-property aspect to the multipurpose resource issue – make isolation strategies impractical except for local trials.

Nevertheless the initial results of these experiments were encouraging and it was decided to move on to *phosphate stripping*: precipitation of phosphate by applying ferrous sulphate at sewage treatment plants, to reduce amounts of nutrient entering the water. The first scheme was introduced on the river Ant above Barton Broad. By 1985 phosphate was down from 350 to a target 100 micrograms per litre, and phytoplankton declined by 50%. Even so plants did not return. Evidently they survive in such water, but once removed do not re-establish. To combat the problem Brian Moss is experimenting with improvised alder twig refuges on Barton Broad. The idea is to provide a habitat for water fleas and protection from their fish predators, in the expectation that the fleas will graze down the phytoplankton. In the meantime stripping has also been introduced on the Bure with the hope that plants will prove easier to bring back because that river has never been so highly eutrophied as the Ant. There is also an associated major new pumping programme over four hectares of the fourteen-hectare Hoveton Little Broad, near Wroxham.

Management issues

According to conventional wisdom, resource management in a democratic pluralist system is about an open bureaucracy that is responsive to the public interest. The actual process is rather more circumscribed. Conservation is not free; it must be paid for by investment now to protect the future availability of resources. Nor is it value free. The initial pressure to investigate the changing ecology of the Broads came from conservationists prepared to fight because their values were offended. Their cause found official expression in the Nature Conservancy Council (NCC), a statutory grant-in-aid body responsible for overseeing nature conservation in Great Britain. There was an energetic Regional Officer of the NCC who felt very strongly about the importance of the Broads, and from its small budget the NCC funded the first work by Brian Moss. The Anglian Water Authority (AWA) with responsibility for water quality was not tackling the problem because the role of sewage effluent in the degradation of the Broads was not fully understood. The AWA argued that it was responsible for public funds and obliged to be certain of the scientific 'facts' before spending on the problem, yet it did not welcome the research. As with the acid rain issue, environmentalists saw this argument as a blocking tactic.

When the first results of Brian Moss's research became available, the NCC was able to press the AWA, and to some extent other local authorities, to face responsibilities. In effect the NCC's bargaining strategy was to use its official standing, and a relatively small amount of money, to make a political investment in conservation that led to subsequent costs being forced elsewhere. Ultimately, the phosphate stripping programme shows how a polluter can be forced to internalise social and environmental costs. It is interesting to notice that the various parties have worked out their bargain around the rapidly accumulating 'objective' scientific evidence when conservationists' values are in the ascendency.

Although these new water pollution control policies may be seen as an important victory for environmental interests, many would argue that truly 'sustainable development' of resources like the Broads will only be achieved when the actual use of phosphates and nitrates is controlled. The present approach treats the symptoms rather than the cause.

Recreation and tourism

The Broads lend themselves to many different types of recreation and holiday activity including wildfowling, naturalist pursuits, water skiing and team rowing, but are mainly renowned for coarse fishing and

An old railway poster extolling the attractions of a holiday on the Norfolk Broads.

NORFOLK

‹LNER›   ‹LNER›

TRAVEL BY RAIL

Anglers and boat users share the same recreational resource.

various types of sailing and cruising. Although people did sail in Broadland for pleasure from around 1840, the area was generally regarded as bleak and remote. Later in the 19th century, The Broads were *discovered* by an upper-middle-class clientele, drawn during the summer months to sailing and the remarkable wetland environment. The contemporary writings of G.C. Davies,[3] particularly his boys' adventure stories, helped to popularise the area, but it was the railways, simultaneously heralding the demise of the commercial wherry and the expansion of tourism, that really opened up the Broads.

In its own commercial interests the Great Eastern Railway Company promoted the area, providing information on boating holidays and running its own pleasure steamer from Wroxham. Loynes Ltd, established in 1878, was the first firm to offer hire cruising, though by modern standards the industry operated on a small scale. In the 1920s there were about 160 yachts and 20 pleasure wherries (some complete with piano!), and the first motor cruisers began to appear. By 1939 there were 100,000 holidaymakers per year, but since the late 1940s the hire fleet has quadrupled in size and with the general introduction of annual paid holidays, the social background of visitors has widened considerably. There are now about 1,750 hire motor cruisers (the peak was 2,200 around 1980) and 100 cruising yachts providing for approximately 200,000 visitors per year, and the once short season now extends from May to October. There is even a demand at Christmas.

Table 6.1 Characteristics of Broadland's users

	Match anglers	Casual anglers	Hire boat users	Motor cruiser owners	Yacht owners
No. of respondents	143	141	211	131	142
			Percentage		
Age					
0–19	13	30	8	1	1
20–29	25	31	31	9	6
30–44	37	22	30	24	33
45–59	23	16	30	44	43
60 and over	2	2	2	22	16
Education					
To minimum leaving age	86	88	79	73	52
17 or 18	12	11	10	18	23
Some higher education	2	2	11	10	25
Social class					
I	1	1	5	14	26
II	8	18	20	41	46
IIIN	20	18	20	19	18
IIIM	38	31	25	19	5
IV	25	25	23	7	5
V	8	7	7	0	0
Area of origin					
East Anglia	97	71	4	59	73
Other	3	29	96	41	27

The area also has a long history of angling and although it is not so easy to know how many anglers use the Broads, they probably number around 90,000 per year.

Not surprisingly, as the popularity of Broadland increased, competition for its resources intensified, users found themselves forced into more interaction with each other, and conflicts emerged which by the late 1970s had become quite serious. Besides the sheer intensity of use, other preconditions of conflict became apparent. There are marked social class and educational differences between groups of users and it is reasonable to expect them to have different views, values and expectations about recreational use of the Broads. This is in fact the case. The huge popularity of angling and boating belies the existence of several types of anglers and boat users who, importantly, are dissimilar kinds of people (Table 6.1) who have rather different goals and objectives in their chosen recreation. The conflicts are made worse because an uneven distribution of use produces particularly intensive interactions at peak times and in certain popular places. Most of the pressure is on the northern river system, which is the most prized resource ecologically, and for its scenery, its land-based and boating facilities (especially for sailing on the open broads), and opportunities for fishing. All is made worse at weekends, for not only is this when most people visit the Broads, but most of the hire boats are based on the northern rivers, and Saturday is the changeover day for holidaymakers. On this day, almost the whole hire fleet first re-groups and then disperses, causing serious congestion.

Fig. 6.5 Network of conflict in the Norfolk Broads.

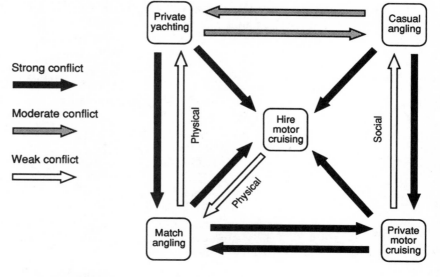

Strong conflict

Moderate conflict

Weak conflict

At one level the potential for conflict between anglers and boat users is obvious because the physical requirements for their activities mean that it is easy for them to get in each other's way. But a closer look at the problem has shown that the conflicts are far deeper and are not simply a function of the number and density of users at any particular place or time. On the contrary, research has shown that the greatest conflict is felt by the most experienced or committed Broads users, regardless of conditions when they were actually questioned. Feeling dissatisfied seems to depend much more on *how often* a day in the Broads has been disrupted by other users, and once bad feelings develop they tend to persist. Over the years the interplay of physical and social factors has produced a complex network of conflict (Fig. 6.5) that presents a real challenge for management.

The strongest feelings are directed against hirers and hire motor cruisers, but the hirers themselves are generally tolerant of other use. Anglers, for example, find hire boating particularly upsetting, but it is by and large a one-way conflict where the hirers are able to transfer their effect (an externality) without themselves being inconvenienced. It would be wrong, however, to assume that conflict is always the consequence of one group being able to impose itself on another simply because of its equipment or method of travel. Several groups of Broads users highlight *social* differences between themselves and others, as in the case of yacht owners and anglers where the mobile yacht owners are actually more bothered by the degree of contact than anglers. In other cases the conflicts are two-way between match (competition) anglers and private cruiser owners, for instance, but neither group can do much to limit the other's use of the common property resource, for in the Broads, Common Law protects both fishing and navigation rights. All such conflicts impair the satisfaction that people can gain from enjoying resources like the Norfolk Broads.

Resolving conflicts

One response might be simply to allow current trends to develop, but an alternative view is that there is a duty positively to manage resources for recreation. Few would argue with a generally expressed goal in resource management: to maximise visitors' satisfaction while at the same time protecting the renewable resource. But deciding on the type and balance of use and enforcing the decision through management is no easy matter. At one extreme the conflicts could be viewed as self-limiting, but without positive management the northern rivers might become dominated by the least sensitive users and suffer increasing pressure from unabated boat traffic. Others would continue to be displaced into more marginal places or times. Is that the way to consume an otherwise unique and renewable resource? One alternative would be to introduce *time and space zoning* to limit use, but it is necessary to be aware that more specialised and conflict-sensitive users may then seek limits that increase their own satisfaction by unfairly imposing costs (a higher chance of exclusion) on others. Deciding the appropriate balance is a managerial issue and there are choices to be made about whether to provide for high or low use, for the mass or the few.

There are many factors to consider. For example, some types of recreation are highly *resource dependent* and the lack of comparable resources – the linked series of open water lakes for yachting, for instance – adds to the *resource pull* of the Broads. Others, such as anglers, are less dependent on this specific resource, but are more numerous and use the area on more days per year. One argument is that, on a national basis, resources should be managed to preserve the whole range of recreation opportunities. 'Low-grade' resources would then be reserved for general and intensive use and scarcer 'high-grade' resources would be available for more specialised and less intensive use. In the context of the Broads this raises another interesting issue: boat users are mainly non-local, and management may need to decide whether to emphasise opportunities for boating, or protect the interests of local anglers.

To a large extent the managerial issues have been academic as far as the Broads are concerned. There is a Common Law right to navigate the tidal waters, and the few powers that do exist to manage the problem are dispersed between different statutory authorities. This has meant that in practice, recreational use has more or less been treated as a self-limiting problem and over the years the conflicts have intensified and the physical environment has been severely degraded because of overuse. We now turn to the third kind of resource use conflict affecting the Broads.

Halvergate

In 1978 a new organisation – the Broads Authority – was formed and in 1980 it was catapulted into a deep controversy that set agricultural land drainage and environmental interests against each other.[4] This case study is an excellent example of the way in which renewable resource management involves conflicts of interest that are resolved by bargaining power and political struggle between competitive groups. The dispute centres on Halvergate Marshes (Fig. 6.1), which extend over several thousand hectares, mainly between the lower Bure and Yare rivers. When the conflict erupted it was difficult to imagine a less

(a) Halvergate landscape, and (b) new drainage works in progress.

a

b

likely tract of land to change the course of public debate about agriculture and countryside policies. Halvergate, although drained, is a *high*-water-table marsh used to graze cattle, sheep and horses. It is a flat and relatively featureless expanse – bleak, windswept and unwelcoming in winter, and even in good weather frustrating to walkers who must negotiate numerous ditches and dykes. Yet Halvergate is a very special and important landscape; it is the last remaining extensive grazing marsh in eastern England and can only survive as long as traditional *low-intensity farming* is sustained.

In 1980 the Lower Bure, Acle Marshes and Halvergate Fleet Internal Drainage Board proposed new *deep* drainage schemes. Farmers – who dominated the Board and enjoyed absolute property rights – recognised a financial interest in installing powerful new pumps so that the marsh could be converted to arable. They wanted to take advantage of artificially high intervention prices available through the Common Agricultural Policy (CAP) of the European Community (EC). Environmentalists were appalled by the proposals, for landscape and amenity reasons, and promoted their own values in the name of the public interest. They argued that it was absurd to allow the market distortions of the CAP to destroy the marshes; agricultural 'profitability' would be enhanced but only because a public subsidy was available to buy-in the crop despite an existing huge cereals surplus. Even so, 'Halvergate' might have remained a purely local conflict but for the coincidence that the Wildlife and Countryside Bill (enacted in 1981) was near to the end of its course through Parliament. The Bill was extremely contentious and the ramifications of the Halvergate drainage proposals in a wider political context were obvious to leading conservationists. They saw an opportunity to embarrass the Government by highlighting important contradictions between its agriculture and countryside policies that worked against conservation and common sense. Halvergate burst on the national scene.

The line-up on opposing sides was formidable (Fig. 6.6), and the two could not have been further apart. The conservationists' fundamental point was that it would be better to pay farmers to produce and sustain countryside by subsidising the traditional farming regime than to turn the land over to cereals that nobody wanted. Yet it was difficult to see how conservationists could press their case, because at that stage Halvergate seemed no more than a local issue, and they were up against a straitjacket imposed by national policies. The Ministry of Agriculture,

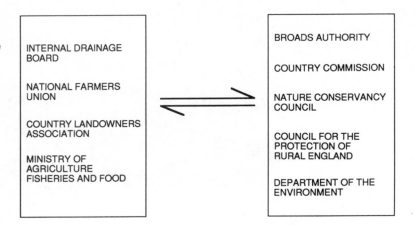

Fig. 6.6 Halvergate: a conflict between agricultural land drainage and conservation interests.

INTERNAL DRAINAGE BOARD

NATIONAL FARMERS UNION

COUNTRY LANDOWNERS ASSOCIATION

MINISTRY OF AGRICULTURE FISHERIES AND FOOD

BROADS AUTHORITY

COUNTRY COMMISSION

NATURE CONSERVANCY COUNCIL

COUNCIL FOR THE PROTECTION OF RURAL ENGLAND

DEPARTMENT OF THE ENVIRONMENT

Fisheries and Food (MAFF) and its clients, on the other hand, felt buttressed by government and EC policies and held firmly to the view that conservation was only acceptable if it did not interfere with 'efficiency'. The MAFF remained determined to defend production incentive payments and land 'improvement'.

The drainage interests began in a strong position. They saw no reason why farmers should not accept cereals subsidies unless the conservationists could offer something better to maintain the status quo. This intransigence and apparent willingness to begin ploughing placed tremendous pressure on conservationists – so much so that their camp was plunged into disarray. The Broads Authority, still in its infancy, felt a particular need to find a solution and tried to negotiate voluntary compensation arrangements for farmers prepared to continue with grazing. The Authority had little room for manoeuvre, but it was here that national political considerations began to have a significant bearing on the Halvergate problem.

The trouble with the Authority's approach was that it would amount to a double payment. Farmers would be paid not to take up subsidies on crops that could only be grown once other subsidies had been spent on new drainage. The Broads Authority was relying on the Countryside Commission to underwrite most of the cost, but the Commission became increasingly uneasy. It did not want any local precedent capable of increasing the cost of conservation nationally, and it felt particularly exposed because it was fighting (with other conservation organisations) to have similar double compensation provisions deleted from the Wildlife and Countryside Bill. Meanwhile the Nature Conservancy Council went its own way and began the process of declaring a Site of Special Scientific Interest[5] over part of the marshes. In the end there was squabbling amongst farmers about how to share the compensation, the national debate intensified and the Broads Authority scheme collapsed, leaving the marshes more under threat than ever and the conservationists out of step with each other.

To make matters worse, the Wildlife and Countryside Act 1981 did after all provide for management agreements based on the principle of compensation for 'profit' forgone. It was reckoned that within ten years the effect might be to suck around 30% of the Broads Authority's annual budget into payments to bribe farmers not to grow crops already in overproduction. Of course, from the farmers' point of view the generous provisions in the new Act seemed to vindicate the stance of drainage interests against the Broads Authority. There was impasse, but in 1984 two things happened to transform the politics of the dispute.

First the Countryside Commission realised that the new compensation arrangements appealed to only a few large farmers. Smaller farmers, by far the majority on Halvergate, were cautious lest they be forced to sell, or switch to arable. The Commission came forward with an innovative experimental scheme – The Broads Grazing Marsh Conservation Scheme – to run from 1985 to 1987. Compensation was offered at a flat rate of £124 per hectare, compared with £250–£400 per hectare under the 'compensation for profit forgone' arrangements, yet 90% of farmers participated and by 1986 the scheme was being used temporarily to protect 6,267 hectares of marsh. Second, milk quotas were imposed by the EC in a move intended to end farmers' expectation of huge subsidies in the face of massive food surpluses. The National Farmers' Union needed a new national strategy on farmers' incomes and in a complete about-face saw that conservation could be taken on board, with new support schemes to offset the loss of production incentive payments. The MAFF co-operated with the Countryside Commission jointly to administer the Broads' experimental scheme and the Government, now with the support of both conservationists and farming interests, persuaded the EC to accept this type of scheme more generally. European Community legislation was passed to enable agriculture ministries to designate *Environmentally Sensitive Areas* in which financial incentives are provided to encourage farming compatible with conservation and amenity considerations. The Broads were selected as an Environmentally Sensitive Area in July 1986 and, unlikely as it may have seemed at the outset, Halvergate came to mark a turning-point: power in the politics of agriculture and the countryside began to move away from the high-tech intensification of agribusiness towards conservation of habitat and landscape. It is an interesting example of an essentially local issue giving a crucial impetus to national – and international – legislation.

Management of the Broads

All of these conflicts demonstrate that the Norfolk Broads are beset by the most serious multipurpose resource problems. How did it happen? Here again we must look beyond a narrow focus on specific problems and consider management of the Broads more generally. When the National Parks of England and Wales were chosen in 1947, Sir Arthur Hobhouse recommended that the Broads be included, but designation did not proceed because, in contrast to the upland areas for which the 1949 National Parks Act was designed, Broadland was relatively small, was not remote or sparsely populated, and had a thriving economy based on intensive farming. Most important of all, the Broads, being essentially a waterscape much used for fishing and boating, presented a different sort of legislative and managerial problem. Broadland was left in limbo and while decline set in there followed *forty years* of bitter wrangling over control and responsibility for management that brought the Broads to the brink of ruin.

Over the years there were several inquiries into the problems of the

Table 6.2 History of non-decision-making in Broadland

Date	Policy	Response	Environmental change
1945	Government Committee of Inquiry into National Parks (The Dower Report). Broads Conference held by local bodies responsible for the Broads.	Dower considers 'Broads National Park' and Conference organisers realise their role might change.	Prolific phase 2 flora and fauna; weed cutting necessary to maintain navigable channels.
1946	**Broads Conference Report** presented.	Recommends new executive authority (a national park?). Conference opts instead for promise of greater co-operation between local bodies.	
1949	National Parks and Access to the Countryside Act.	Broads selected as possible national park.	Environmental decline noticeable.
1955	National Parks Commission considers designating a Broads National Park.	Designation withheld for lack of scientific survey of Broadland's problems, but will not fund study.	Rapid environmental change obvious. Detergent-rich effluent now discharged. Broads increasingly popular.
1961–65	Nature Conservancy survey and report on Broadland.	Includes call for new executive authority, but instead local bodies form a 'Consortium'.	Ecological changes not understood but parallel fourfold increase in hire fleet noted.
1966	**Broads Consortium** set up.	Norfolk County Planning Officer to prepare a Broadland Study and Plan.	
1968	Countryside Act.	Countryside Commission created to oversee landscape conservation and recreation in the countryside.	Most rivers and broads reach fully impoverished phase 3 condition.
1971	**Broadland Study and Plan** published.	Again, new executive authority recommended, but rejected – especially by Rivers Commissioners who would lose their powers to new authority.	Impasse; broads deteriorate still further.
1976–80	**Countryside Commission** intervenes and first Broads Authority formed by local bodies to pre-empt national park designation.	Broads Authority begins to prepare a **Strategy and Management Plan for Broadland**.	Ecological research (e.g. on Cockshoot Broad) begins to unravel process of eutrophication. Significant recreation conflicts and voluntary zoning of users on part of river Ant.
1983	Countryside Commission decides to press for new legislation to provide Broads Authority with executive powers.	Publicity and success surrounding Broads Authority mean local bodies can no longer resist radical changes in management.	Phosphate stripping in place to relieve Barton Broad. New speed restrictions on boat traffic imposed. Halvergate is dominant issue.
1986–89	Norfolk and Suffolk Broads Act passed and second **Broads Authority** formed.	Priority of new executive Authority is restoration of the Broads.	Environmentally Sensitive Area status won. Restoration schemes extended to Hoveton and Belaugh Broads.

Broads (Table 6.2). These were apparently intended to provide an understanding of the interplay of human and physical factors with a view to recommending specific resource management programmes, but the conclusions reached invariably pointed to a more fundamental political issue: statutory organisation was ineffective and needed to be altered if there was to be successful resource management. In 1945, spurred on by the country's initiative on national parks, Norfolk County Council convened the Broads Conference. The Conference concluded that proper management called for a single executive authority, but the move was abandoned because legislation resulting in the 'transfer of statutory functions from County, District and Parish Councils to an entirely new body would involve strenuous opposition from the existing authorities'. Instead it was decided simply to rely on more active and co-ordinated use of existing powers. Debate about a national park did rumble on until 1961, but came to nothing.

The Government then asked the Nature Conservancy to consider Broadland's problems. Its 1965 report reiterated many of the administrative arguments which by then had been around for twenty years. A strongly worded supplement called for a new authority linked to national administration, but instead, in view of the 'urgency' of the situation, it was decided to form a Consortium of local bodies to co-ordinate matters and prepare (another) plan relating to the future of Broadland! The opportunity to press for a new body passed into the background: it would take time and meet significant local political opposition. In 1971 the Norfolk County Planning Officer reported to the consortium and again recommended a new authority, this time with the elaboration that it should be a planning authority responsible also for navigation. But the navigation authority – the Rivers Yare, Bure and Waveney Commissioners – objected to both proposals and managed to remain independent.

This history of inaction is an excellent example of non-decision-making (see Chapter 2). By 1971 there existed three major reports, all produced by essentially the same collection of local interests. Taken in isolation, successive conclusions about ecological problems and the desirability of redistributing statutory responsibilities made each seem entirely reasonable. But as the decades passed the ploy of repeatedly studying the problems of the Broads was revealed as a delaying tactic that protected local interests and the status quo. The authorities involved were publicly proclaiming despair over the decline of the Broads when, as if drifting under the spell of a New Columbus Syndrome,[6] from time to time they 'discovered' the multipurpose use problems. The point that was conveniently left on one side was that the problems were *worse* rather than different, and worse largely because statutory re-organisation had not been faced head-on. Finally, in 1976 the Countryside Commission stepped in and, shortcomings in the legislation notwithstanding, recommended a new National Park Authority with navigation powers. This option again proved politically unacceptable locally, and local bodies sought to head off the Commission's initiative by establishing a Broads Authority; the Commission held off national park designation for the time being, but required a Strategy and Management Plan to be prepared! The Commission knew what was wrong, but was outmanoeuvred when local statutory organisations closed ranks to recycle their well-rehearsed 'solution' to a potential attack on their own powers.

The Broads Authority, set up in 1978, was a joint advisory (not executive) committee whose members included representatives from the ten statutory authorities with interests in the area, together with three Countryside Commission nominees. Planning and countryside powers were delegated to it by the local authorities concerned, but neither the Water Authority nor the Rivers Commissioners were able to delegate powers. This last point is crucial. The Broads Authority remained dependent on co-operation and co-ordination with water and navigation interests and still lacked the powers that had been wanting for several decades.

'A better future'

Subsequent changes in management of the Broads hold out far more promise that decline can be reversed. In effect the Broads Authority became a new player amongst the interests previously dominant in the politics of Broadland, and changed the balance of power. Once there is a new bureaucracy, an ethos develops within it concerned with maintaining and promoting the role of the organisation as a whole. When it was established, the Broads Authority had a most uncertain future and its professional staff were acutely aware of their need to do all that they could to secure its long-term prospects. To some extent the Authority's role in the Halvergate affair reflects such organisational imperatives. Halvergate could have killed off the Broads Authority at an early stage, but its effect, together with a general surge in national concern with conservation and countryside issues, was to confirm its role. The momentum of events gave the Broads such a high profile that it became impossible even for Norfolk's well-practised local bodies to keep the Broads off the national political agenda. The success of the new authority and the high public profile that it came to enjoy made it possible for the Countryside Commission to seek special legislation to provide it with greater powers. The *Norfolk and Suffolk Broads Bill* received an unopposed second reading in 1986. The Broads Authority, which came into existence on 5th April 1989, has been set up almost exactly along the lines suggested over forty years ago. It is a national park in all but name and has direct control over navigation within its executive area.

In recent years, conflicts between agriculture and conservation have tended to overshadow recreation problems, because the former have been more pressing, while powers to deal with the latter have been unsatisfactory. But the popularity of the Broads will almost certainly increase as further environmental improvement takes place. Furthermore, the prominence and status of the new Authority seem bound to bring the area to the attention of an even wider market, making sustainable management of the renewable resources of Broadland even more important. As this chapter has shown, the new authority will have to balance many competing claims on the Broads environment. The success of this process – involving politics at least as much as science – will determine whether Broadland survives as a unique environment to be used sustainably and enjoyed by future generations.

7 Achievements and prospects

We began in Chapter 1 by noting the great upsurge in environmental concern that has occurred since the 1960s. Now, in the final chapter, we assess the impacts of this revolution, evaluate its achievements and consider the prospects for resolving environmental problems in the future.

The impact of environmentalism can be measured in three rather different ways. First we can consider the stimulation of *awareness* of environmental issues in government, in other organisations and among the public at large. Then we can look at the extent to which changing social values and priorities have been translated into *actual policies* by governments and international organisations. Finally, we can assess the impact on the *environment itself*. Have problems been solved? Is there better provision for environmental protection? Has environmental quality been improved or at least maintained? These must be the ultimate criteria for success. Awareness of problems makes little difference if environmentally destructive activities continue unchallenged, and legislation is of limited use unless it is implemented and effective in achieving its ends. Changing awareness, changing policies and the state of the environment itself are all considered in this chapter, though most emphasis must be on policies and legislation, since these provide the most tangible, if not an entirely adequate, measure of the impact of the 'environmental revolution'.

A new awareness

The emergence of the modern environmental movement was itself a product of increasing awareness of the human impact on the environment, but initially this was restricted to a rather small section of the population. Two decades of campaigning, conflict, the physical reality of environmental degradation and the constant attention of the media have helped to diffuse environmental consciousness much more widely among the public, policy-makers, industry and other institutions, to the extent that some opinion polls now suggest that environmental problems are perceived second only to a superpower conflict as the 'greatest threat' to the human race (for example, a Gallup poll conducted in Britain in autumn 1988). Such widespread concern about pollution and conservation makes the claim that environmentalism is 'elitist' less convincing. While it is true that membership of pressure groups such as the Council for the Protection of Rural England (CPRE) or Friends of the Earth (FOE) is still dominated by better-off and better educated people, several studies have revealed widespread passive support for active groups among the public as a whole: Philip Lowe and Jane Goyder refer to 'the attentive public'.[1] Opinion polls, though their results must be treated with some caution, tend to confirm this finding,

The preservation of wildlife and the environment is a major concern of Esso and we therefore wish the British Wildlife Appeal every success.

(Esso)

Beautifuel Gas!

Clean air and unspoilt countryside–from the Gas People.

Corporate advertisements. Industry is anxious to display its green credentials.

Table 7.1   Public attitudes to environmental issues (percentage figures)

Priority	1982	1985	1988
Protect the environment	50	60	74
Keep prices down	40	23	17
Don't know	10	17	9

Percentage placing environmental protection ahead of economic growth:
1986   55%
1988   70%

Source: Environmental Data Services Report 166, November 1988: figures from Gallup poll conducted for *The Daily Telegraph* in October 1988.

suggesting a growing concern with many aspects of environmental quality. The Gallup poll mentioned above found that a large majority of respondents (a higher proportion than in previous polls) claimed to place environmental protection *ahead* of economic objectives (Table 7.1) and a substantial minority (15%) said that they had boycotted products of companies that they felt were environmentally irresponsible. The potency of 'green consumerism', as opposed to direct environmental conflict at the other end of the production process, is only just beginning to be recognised by environmental groups and industry alike. When *The Green Consumer Guide*[2] was published in September 1988, the first printing of 25,000 copies and most of the next 15,000 had been sold within a fortnight. There can be little doubt that environmental awareness among the general public and, perhaps more significantly, willingness to translate this awareness into action, have reached unprecedented levels.

There has also been a noticeable 'greening' in political circles, as politicians respond to pressure from environmental groups and to public opinion, and often from the international and scientific communities as well. In Britain the major political parties have been vying with each other, especially during the latter part of the 1980s, to be seen to have the best environmental credentials, and have devoted increasing space to the environment in policy statements, manifestos and speeches. The response is similar in other countries: in 1988 the environment was the dominant issue in the Swedish general election, and in the autumn of the same year the three most influential global leaders – Mrs Thatcher in an address to the Royal Society, Mr Bush during the presidential election and Mr Gorbachev in a speech to the UN General Assembly – all highlighted the urgency of dealing with global environmental problems. The gulf between rhetoric and real commitment to action is often very wide, but the increasingly prominent position of environmental issues on the political agenda is at least a sign that an important pre-condition for action has been achieved.

It is perhaps inevitable, as the environmentalist Tom Burke has argued, that:

> the elevation of environmental issues to the mainstream political agenda also lifts their prominence as a feature of the business environment.[3]

A Green Party view of the 'greening' of British politics in the mid-1980s. Political parties all over Europe have become more acutely aware of environmental concerns in the 1980s; in June 1989 their awareness was reinforced by dramatic gains for green parties in the elections to the European Parliament.

Source: The Green Party.

In other words, there has been a 'greening' of industry too. This conversion is not entirely altruistic. Progressive companies have accepted at last that environmental concern is here to stay, are beginning to recognise the competitive advantages of being environmentally sound, and are shifting markedly from old defensive positions. Companies are deeply conscious of their corporate image, which can influence recruitment, sales, share values and the political climate within which they operate: anxiety that this image should be environmentally benign is now clearly reflected in many corporate advertising campaigns.

The advantages of anticipating and keeping ahead of environmental legislation rather than resisting it to the bitter end are also much more widely acknowledged. This can simply be good business practice: for example, if a new plant is being built, it is often economically efficient to install better pollution control equipment than regulations currently require, in anticipation of the imposition of more stringent controls within the lifetime of the plant. Companies that fail to anticipate environmental opinion and legislation may also lose important markets, especially export markets. For example, cadmium content may determine whether products can be sold in Sweden, and ability to meet emission controls affects the sale of motor vehicles throughout the developed world. On the other hand, companies that lead the field in environmental products and technology stand to take advantage of a rapidly expanding market: by 1985 overseas trade in air pollution control and wastewater treatment equipment was earning European companies around £5 billion a year, and in the United States annual capital and running expenditures for pollution abatement and control were estimated at around $70 billion.[4] The outstanding success of companies like The Body Shop demonstrate the market potential of 'green' consumer products too. So perhaps it is not surprising to find Sir David Nickson, President of the Confederation of British Industry (CBI), arguing that:

> Environmental excellence gives a competitive edge which has to be recognised and incorporated from the start. . . . Disregard of environmental factors leads to inefficiency, misuse of valuable resources and inattention to the needs of the customer – a recipe for failure.[5]

Once again, some caution must be exercised in interpreting this apparent 'greening' of industry and commerce; it is easier to produce glossy corporate policy statements and advertisements than to ensure that environmental consciousness pervades all levels of an organisation, or genuinely to elevate environmental protection to have equal priority with other business objectives. Unfortunately, irresponsible and even illegal practice is still all too commonplace. While many environmentalists cautiously welcome the 'green trend' in industry, and seek to build upon it by identifying opportunities for co-operation, others are unconvinced. The sceptics fear that the environmental movement is being bought off too easily by the concept of 'green growth' and maintain that a lasting solution to environmental problems must involve fundamental change to the system of which industry is itself a part. This brings us back to the question of whether 'green growth' can really be sustained in the indefinite future, and therefore to the problem of defining 'sustainable development': we return to this issue in our assessment of progress and prospects below. First, however, we should examine the extent to which changing values are reflected in the environmental policies of national and international organisations.

Changing policies

Most policies that have an impact on the environment are made at national level. But environmental problems, as the acid rain issue demonstrates all too clearly (Chapter 4), do not respect national boundaries: indeed, many are global in character and require global action for their solution. Even when the problems themselves are not 'transnational', there is an important international dimension to environmental policy because stringent regulations in any one country may make its own industries uncompetitive and international capital may simply shift to 'pollution havens' in less well-regulated parts of the world. It is important therefore to examine both national and international policies for environmental protection.

National policies

In many countries, policies designed to protect the environment have long historical roots. In Britain, for example, by the end of the 19th century there was quite extensive legislation covering air and water pollution, public health and nature conservation. In both the United States and the Soviet Union, laws to protect nature and public health had their origins long before the emergence of the modern environmental movement in the 1960s. Since the 1960s, however, the pace of legislative activity has greatly intensified and its scope has extended widely. During the 1970s, the number of countries with governmental institutions dealing with environmental management grew from 15 to 115. In Britain, the Department of the Environment was established in 1970 and the influential Royal Commission on Environmental Pollution was set up in 1972 to provide independent expert advice to the Government. In the last two decades significant environmental legislation has covered air and water pollution, toxic waste and countryside conservation: some important Acts are listed in Table 7.2. Not only has there been a considerable amount of new legislation, but much greater use has recently been made of existing opportunities for public involvement, as provided, for example, by the Town and Country Planning Acts. Opposition to major development proposals – often extending to criticism of the policies behind them – has been voiced during the planning process, and particularly at public inquiries. This partly explains the length and complexity of inquiries into the nuclear reprocessing plant at Windscale (now Sellafield), proposed mining of coal in the Vale of Belvoir, expansion of Stansted Airport, and construction of Britain's first pressurised water reactor (PWR) at Sizewell. The last inquiry broke all records, sitting for 340 working days and costing in the region of £25 million. None of these inquiries actually resulted in cancellation of the proposed development, but in all cases the project was almost certainly more environmentally sensitive as a result of the scrutiny to which it had been subjected. In the United States, environmental groups have made extensive use of the courts to challenge policies and proposals in a similar way, though they have often been assisted by the framework provided by the National Environmental Policy Act discussed in more detail below (Fig. 7.1).

Few environmental policies are without their critics, who often consider them too weak and implemented with insufficient vigour. The

Table 7.2 Dates of significant post-war legislation concerned with the environment in the UK

Town and Country Planning Act	1947
National Parks and Access to the Countryside Act	1949
Rivers (Prevention of Pollution) Act	1951
Clean Air Act	1956
Countryside Act	1968
Deposit of Poisonous Waste Act	1972
Water Act	1973
Control of Pollution Act	1974
Health and Safety at Work Act	1974
Endangered Species (Import and Export) Act	1976
Wildlife and Countryside Act	1981
Norfolk and Suffolk Broads Act	1986
Water Act	1989

Fig. 7.1 Citizen suits filed under five US environmental statutes, 1978–83.

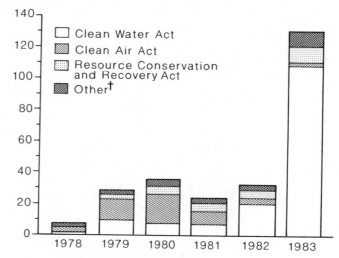

Number of suits or notices of intent*

Clean Water Act
Clean Air Act
Resource Conservation and Recovery Act
Other[†]

Source: US Environmental Law Institute.

* includes notices of intent to file suit as well as suits actually filed

† includes Toxic Substances Control Act, Safe Drinking Water Act, and suits citing more than one of these five statutes.

environmental lobby is certainly not always the most powerful in the policy-making process, and the result is typically a compromise, and rarely a complete victory for environmental interests. Nor does the influence of different groups end with the passing of legislation. When the UK Control of Pollution Act came onto the statute book in 1974, its effectiveness was limited by an agreement that its provisions should not be enforced immediately because of the 'uncertain economic climate': the Act was not fully implemented for more than ten years, and even then many discharges to water remained effectively exempt from its controls.

The environmental lobby has to fight hard, with limited resources, to achieve what it often sees as rather marginal policy adjustments. In some cases, as in its opposition to energy developments, it has hardly succeeded in challenging the basic tenets of policy at all, though it has probably been effective in reducing the environmental impacts of specific developments. Occasionally, however, an issue captures public and media attention in a way that forces rapid policy change. The Poisonous Waste Act 1972 was rushed into the statute book in a matter of weeks after a national newspaper revealed the illegal dumping of drums of cyanide on a tip where children played. In 1983, Greenpeace activists, attempting to block a waste outlet from Sellafield, revealed a large accidental discharge of radioactive waste, the impact of which was reinforced by the subsequent closure of local beaches because of radiation hazard: the resulting scandal succeeded in forcing major reductions in permitted levels of discharge from the plant, where years of sober argument had failed. Such incidents tend to be isolated examples, however, and progress is typically slow, incremental and less spectacular.

In Britain, environmental legislation has tended to proceed in a piecemeal manner. The United States, in contrast, responded to the

Direct action by some environmental groups attracts considerable media attention.

environmental pressures of the 1960s with new and comprehensive legislation – the National Environmental Policy Act, or NEPA. This Act provides an excellent example of the achievements and limitations of national environmental legislation.

The US National Environmental Policy Act

The US National Environmental Policy Act (NEPA) of 1969 is one of the best-known pieces of national environmental legislation. A product of the powerful environmental consciousness which emerged in the US in the 1960s (see Chapter 1), it was far-reaching and radical in concept, especially in a country without a well-developed land use planning and development control system like that of the UK. NEPA sought to raise the profile of environmental considerations in national policy-making. The preamble to the Act places a responsibility on the Federal Government 'to use all practicable means, consistent with other essential considerations of national policy' to

(i)   fulfil the responsibilities of each generation as trustee of the environment for succeeding generations;

(ii) assure for all Americans safe, healthful, productive, and aesthetically and culturally pleasing surroundings;

(iii) attain the widest range of beneficial uses of the environment without degradation, risk to health or safety, or any other undesirable or unintended consequences;

(iv) preserve important historic, cultural and natural aspects of the national heritage, and maintain, wherever possible, an environment which supports diversity, and variety of individual choice;

(v) achieve a balance between population and resource use which will permit high standards of living and a wide sharing of life's amenities; and

(vi) enhance the quality of renewable resources and approach the maximum attainable recycling of depletable resources.

Another important provision of NEPA was that 'major federal actions significantly affecting the quality of the human environment' would be subject to *Environmental Impact Assessment* (EIA) and all proposals for such actions would be accompanied by an *Environmental Impact Statement* (EIS) which would detail, amongst other things, the adverse environmental effects of the proposal. Subsequently the EIA concept has been developed and refined, and applied in many individual states (NEPA was federal legislation) and also in many other countries.

NEPA was undoubtedly very ambitious, but how effective has it been in maintaining and improving the quality of the environment? Its provisions were high-minded, but often vague and subject to widely varying interpretation. The Act itself established an advisory body, the Council on Environmental Quality (CEQ), intended to provide an independent review of progress, but it had only a small staff and no power of veto over proposed actions. However, environmental groups made effective use of litigation to ensure that agencies adhered to the provisions of the new law – so effective, in fact, that the CEQ had to introduce new regulations in 1978 to simplify EISs which had become massive and unwieldy in an attempt to avoid challenge by environmental groups in the courts. Twenty years after NEPA was enacted, it is widely regarded as a 'qualified success' and a number of observers who have followed its progress claim that its EIA provisions at least have made a significant difference to decision-making. As one recent review put it, 'At the US Federal level, impact assessment works'.[6]

Others, however, have questioned the extent to which NEPA has changed priorities, especially where military security, the economy or jobs are at stake. Judith Rees suggests that the 'success' of EIA represents 'at best . . . a marginal shift towards environmentalist demands', and she argues that:

> Although environmental quality and diversity were given statutory recognition as important public policy objectives, the caveats surrounding their achievement left no doubt that economic development was not to be sacrificed in any material way to environmental aspirations.[7]

Although the 'success' of environmental policy must ultimately be judged by its impact on environmental quality, it is important to remember that legislation like NEPA provides an essential framework. Its effectiveness will always depend on the relative priorities of agencies and individuals and the way in which they use and interpret the procedures which the legislation has provided. This is true both of national legislation and of international environmental policy, to which we now turn.

International environmental policy

As with national environmental legislation, international policy-making has intensified since the 1960s, but has long roots. The Commission for the River Rhine, for example, began to function in 1868, and the International Boundary and Water Commission of the United States and Mexico was established in 1889: both were concerned, as many international commissions are today, with transboundary pollution.

Some existing international institutions, for example the United Nations (UN), the Organisation for Economic Co-operation and Development (OECD), and the European Community (EC) have powers that can be brought to bear on the environment, and many new institutions have been established specifically to deal with environmental problems such as transfrontier pollution or the conservation of species and habitat: examples include the Paris and Oslo Commissions concerned with the North Sea, the International Whaling Commission and the Agency established to administer the deep sea bed by the Law of the Sea Treaty.

But there are major problems in the formulation and enforcement of international environmental laws. International agreements, conventions and treaties have to be negotiated, signed and often 'ratified' (approved by the sovereign, or the Parliament of the states involved); often a minimum number of signatories has to ratify the agreement before it can take effect. The whole procedure can take many years, and even when a Convention is at last in force, and therefore binding on all those states that have signed and ratified it, there are few effective sanctions if its provisions are not honoured.

Some international agreements set out broad principles. For example, the much quoted Principles 21 and 22 agreed at the UN Conference on the Human Environment in Stockholm (1972) state that:

> . . . states have . . . the sovereign right to exploit their own resources pursuant to their own environmental policies, and the responsibility to ensure that activities within their jurisdiction or control do not cause damage to the environment of other states or areas beyond the limits of national jurisdiction (Principle 21)

and that:

> . . . states shall cooperate to develop further the international law regarding liability and compensation for victims of pollution and other environmental damage caused by activities within their jurisdiction (Principle 22).

Another example is the principle adopted by the OECD which in effect means that victims of transfrontier pollution should be able to seek a remedy *as if there were no frontier* – though the victim has to prove liability which, as the discussion of acid rain has shown, may be extremely difficult to do. Such principles are mainly honoured in the breach. Of more practical significance is the growing number of more specific bilateral and multilateral agreements, some important examples of which are described in Table 7.3. Konrad von Moltke, an expert on international environmental law, estimates that by the late 1980s there were more than 500 bilateral arrangements and more than 150 multilateral conventions. These figures do not include the legislation of

Table 7.3 A selection of international conventions

WATER

The Rhine Convention
Convention on the protection of the Rhine against chemical pollution

Drawn up by Switzerland, France, West Germany, Luxembourg and the Netherlands to protect the Rhine against pollution; provides for strict control of discharges. Agreed in Bonn, 1976. The European Community has also become a party.

The Strasbourg Convention
Draft European convention for the protection of international watercourses against pollution

Initially drawn up by the Council of Europe in May 1969, but complicated by overlap between its proposals and those in the European Community's own action programme on the environment. Still not adopted.

The Paris Convention
Convention for the prevention of marine pollution from land-based sources

Drawn up in 1974 to prevent pollution of the north-east Atlantic, including the North Sea. Initial signatories were those whose coasts bordered these waters. The EC now participates. The scope has been extended to cover atmospheric inputs to the sea.

Bonn Agreement
Agreement for co-operation in dealing with pollution of the North Sea by oil

Drawn up in 1969 by countries with coasts on the North Sea. Provides for manpower, supplies, equipment and scientific advice in the event of discharges of oil or other noxious or hazardous substances in the North Sea. The EC is now a party.

Oslo Convention
Convention for the prevention of marine pollution by dumping from ships and aircraft

Drawn up in 1972, came into force in 1974. Covers north-east Atlantic. Countries with coasts bordering this area have undertaken to stop dumping certain materials, and only to allow dumping of others with a specific permit.

Barcelona Convention
Convention for the protection of the Mediterranean Sea against pollution

Programme of action drawn up by countries bordering the Mediterranean in 1975 under the United Nations Environment Programme.

Cartagena Convention
Convention for the protection and development of the marine environment of the wider Caribbean region

Similar to Barcelona Convention in respect of wider Caribbean region.

Helsinki Convention
Convention on the protection of the marine environment of the Baltic Sea area

Adopted by several countries bordering the Baltic Sea in 1980. Seeks to control and restrict discharges of harmful substances into the area.

the European Community, which has special characteristics and is considered in more detail below.

The bringing into existence of an international agreement is often a major achievement in itself, but of course it can only declare agreed intentions; whether or not it is effectively implemented is another question. John Carroll, Professor of Environmental Conservation at the University of New Hampshire, USA, has devoted much attention to international agreements. His comments on the International Joint Commission, created by the Boundary Waters Treaty between the United States and Canada, and widely considered to be successful, are revealing:

AIR

Geneva Convention Convention on long-range transboundary air pollution	Drawn up under the auspices of the United Nations Economic Commission for Europe. Adopted in 1979, came into force in 1983. Seeks protection from, and gradual reduction of, air pollution. Provides for exchange of information, research, monitoring and development of policies. A Protocol signed at Helsinki requires parties to reduce emissions of sulphur dioxide by 30% by 1993 (the '30% Club'). The UK has not signed this protocol.
Vienna Convention Convention for the protection of the ozone layer	The first global convention concerned with the atmosphere. The Montreal Protocol, which came into force in 1989, requires countries to cut consumption of chlorofluorocarbons (CFCs).

WILDLIFE

Ramsar Convention Convention on wetlands of international importance especially as waterfowl habitat.	Adopted in 1971, came into force in 1975. Aims to stem encroachment on, and loss of, wetlands.
CITES Convention on International Trade in Endangered Species (Washington)	Drawn up in 1973. Institutes a system of licensing for trade in endangered species, and prevents trade in most endangered species.
Berne Convention Convention on the conservation of European wildlife and natural habitats	Drawn up by Council of Europe in 1979. Seeks to conserve wild flora and fauna in their natural habitats when conservation requires the co-operation of several states.
Bonn Convention Convention on the conservation of migratory species of wild animals	Drawn up in 1979. States within whose borders there are threatened populations of migratory species should take concerted action to ensure conservation and management.

Source: **Haigh, N.** (1987) *EEC Environmental Policy and Britain*, 2nd edition, Longman, London.

> If measured against other similar attempts to achieve bilateral accord in North America or elsewhere, we may certainly say it is successful. And I think most would agree it has been successful in its very narrow technical responsibility in water apportionment at the [US–Canada] border. But in broader societal concerns of water and air pollution, it has achieved little of significance *when measured against getting the problem solved*, and that should be the only real measure.[8]

Similarly, he argues that the Barcelona Convention (concerned with pollution of the Mediterranean), and the related Mediterranean Action Plan of the United Nations Environment Programme, has been

> . . . lauded for the speed of its enactment, the speed of consensus it achieved in moving toward ratification. But what about the bigger environmental problems facing the Mediterranean . . .? This multilateral action plan will secure for us a certain amount of research and monitoring . . ., but will it tackle the really big

problem of non-point source pollution by land based run-off . . .? Will it significantly reduce the continued dumping of raw sewage and industrial effluent from point sources along the coast? There are few signs that it will do so in the near term, and perhaps not in the long term either.[8]

Many of the problems associated with international agreements have been encountered by the European Community in developing an environmental policy applicable to all twelve of its member states. It does have some advantage, however, because European legislation, once enacted, is binding on all member states, and those that fail to implement legislation face an embarrassing appearance before the European Court of Justice. Since the Community's environmental policy is widely regarded as successful, at least in terms of 'consciousness raising' and legislative activity, it is worth considering it in some detail as an example of the international approach.

The environmental policy of the European Community

The Treaty of Rome, signed by the original six member states in 1957, had no provision for environmental policy, and it was not until the early 1970s – another result of the 'environmental revolution' – that the Community began to turn its attention to environmental affairs. At a summit meeting in Paris in October 1972, Community leaders made the following declaration:

> . . . economic expansion is not an end in itself: its first aim should be to enable disparities in living conditions to be reduced . . . It should result in an improvement in the quality of life as well as in standards of living. As befits the genius of Europe, particular attention will be given to intangible values and to protecting the environment so that progress may really be put at the service of mankind.

A Community 'Action Programme' on the environment was called for, and a new Environment and Consumer Protection Service was established at the EC headquarters in Brussels, though without the status or the resources of a full Directorate-General.

Since then, European environmental policy has matured and developed and many believe that it has had a significant impact on the policies of member states (of which there are now twelve). It is based on thirteen principles, summarised in Table 7.4, which have underpinned a series of Environmental Action Programmes (the fourth covering the period 1987–92). However, there has been a significant shift of emphasis over the fifteen years of EC environmental policy from essentially remedial, 'clean-up' action to a preventative, precautionary and anticipatory approach. The Environment and Consumer Protection Service was 'upgraded' in 1981 to a full Directorate-General for Environment, Consumer Protection and Nuclear Safety. It has certainly made its presence felt in the Community.

Since 1973, around 200 items of legislation have been adopted in the environmental field, dealing with many aspects of pollution, nature conservation and environmental protection. The most common instrument of European environmental policy has been the Directive,

Table 7.4   Principles of European Community environmental policy

1 The best environmental policy consists in preventing the creation of pollution at source rather than subsequently trying to counter their effects.
2 Environmental policy can and must be compatible with economic and social development.
3 Effect on the environment should be taken into account at the earliest possible stage in all technical planning and decision-making processes.
4 Any exploitation of natural resources or anything which causes significant damage to the ecological balance must be avoided.
5 Standards of scientific and technological knowledge in the Community should be improved with a view to taking effective action to conserve and improve the environment and combat pollution and nuisances. Research in this field should therefore be encouraged.
6 The cost of preventing and eliminating nuisances must in principle be borne by the polluter.
7 Care should be taken to ensure that activities carried out in one State do not cause any degradation of the environment in another State.
8 The Community and its Member States must take account in their environmental policy of the interests of the developing countries, and must in particular examine any repercussions of the measures contemplated under that policy on the economic development of such countries.
9 The Community and the Member States must make their voices heard in international organisations dealing with aspects of the environment and must make an original contribution to these organisations.
10 The protection of the environment is a matter for all in the Community, who should therefore be made aware of its importance.
11 In each different category of pollution, it is necessary to establish the level of action that befits the type of pollution.
12 Major aspects of environmental policy in individual countries must no longer be planned and implemented in isolation.
13 Community environmental policy is aimed, as far as possible, at the co-ordinated and harmonised progress of national policies, without, however, hampering potential or actual progress at the national level. However, the latter should be carried out in a way that does not jeopardise the satisfactory operation of the common market.

Source: **Commission of the European Communities** (1987), *The European Community and the Environment* (3rd edition), European Documentation 3/1987, Office for Official Publications of the European Community.

an agreed policy which is binding as to the results to be achieved, but leaves member states to choose the method of implementation. Important legislation likely to have a major impact on British pollution control policy includes the 'large combustion plant' Directive (see Chapter 4), and a series of directives on hazardous waste, water pollution and vehicle emissions. In the spirit of preventative action, and drawing on the American experience of NEPA, a major Directive was adopted in 1986 (implemented from July 1988) which makes environmental impact assessment (EIA) mandatory for certain types of development in all member states.

Negotiation over European legislation is often protracted and acrimonious because economic and environmental interests are intricately bound together, and agreement on many environmental policies has required unanimity in the Council of Ministers. This is why the 'large combustion plant' Directive took five years to negotiate, the EIA Directive was re-drafted seventeen times and agreement on vehicle emissions has been slow and difficult. In the face of such obstacles it is a remarkable achievement that EC environmental policy has covered so much ground since 1973.

The record in terms of implementation is rather less encouraging, which is why implementation of legislation was given priority in the Fourth Action Programme on the Environment. Another important priority for this programme – and now a requirement under the Single European Act – is the *integration* of an environmental dimension into all other major policy areas of the Community, which will certainly be a major challenge for international environmental policy, very much in the spirit of the World Conservation Strategy and the Brundtland Report, discussed in Chapter 1.

A better environment?

The development of environmental consciousness and environmental legislation over the past few decades have been dramatic. Does this mean that the problems are being solved – that the environment is, in fact, getting better? Although the state of the environment must be the true measure of success, it is also the most elusive, not least because of the sheer problems of monitoring environmental quality and establishing trends over time. There is no complete and authoritative series of data on the state of the global environment, though valuable information is provided by, for example, the Worldwatch Institute's annual *State of the World* Report,[9] and by *World Resources*, published annually by the World Resources Institute and the International

National Environmental Survey produced by the Netherlands National Institute of Public Health and Environmental Protection. The report will be used as a basis for environmental policy in the Netherlands in the 1990s.

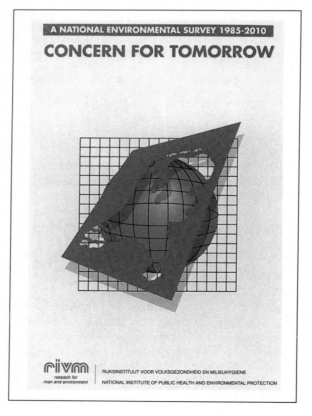

A NATIONAL ENVIRONMENTAL SURVEY 1985-2010

CONCERN FOR TOMORROW

riivm
*reseach for
man and environment*

RIJKSINSTITUUT VOOR VOLKSGEZONDHEID EN MILIEUHYGIENE

NATIONAL INSTITUTE OF PUBLIC HEALTH AND ENVIRONMENTAL PROTECTION

Institute for Environment and Development.[10] 'State of the environment' reports can also now be found for a number of individual countries.

Most of these reports point to similar conclusions. As Tom Burke argues:

> New problems have emerged faster than old ones have been remedied. Whilst some of the grossest environmental abuses have been reduced in some regions, most notably North America and Western Europe, in much of the rest of the world, new problems have simply been piled on top of the old.[3]

Certainly, in developed countries like Europe and North America there *has* been significant progress in dealing with many pollution problems, especially urban air pollution, as Figs 7.2–7.4 demonstrate. There has

Fig. 7.2   US trends in ambient air quality for five pollutants, 1975–84.

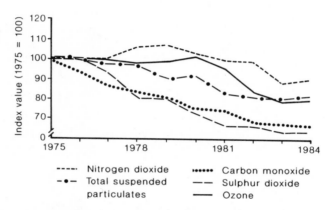

- - - - -   Nitrogen dioxide
- •-   Total suspended particulates
•••••   Carbon monoxide
- -   Sulphur dioxide
———   Ozone

Source: US Environmental Protection Agency.

Fig. 7.3   Smoke emissions from coal combustion, and average urban concentrations in the UK.

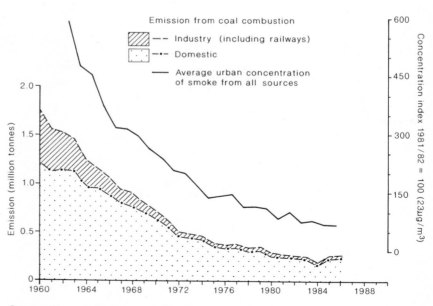

Source: Warren Spring Laboratory, Department of Trade and Industry.

Fig. 7.4 Estimated emissions of lead in the UK.

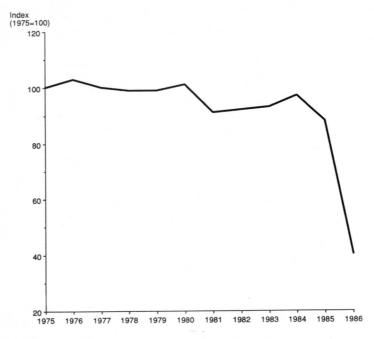

Index (1975=100)

Source: Warren Spring Laboratory, Department of Trade and Industry.

Notes: The emissions are from petrol-driven road vehicles only. Emissions of lead fell by over 60% between 1975 and 1986 owing to reduction of lead in petrol, despite an increase of 33% in motor spirit consumption over the same period.

been progress in other areas too: new chemical substances entering the environment are now subject to stringent testing and approval procedures, and some of the most persistent and toxic substances have been withdrawn (Fig. 7.5); international agreement has been reached to phase out ozone-damaging chlorofluorocarbons and in many countries a more anticipatory approach to environmental policy, as in Environmental Impact Assessment, should reduce negative impacts of many industrial and infrastructural developments in future.

But for every success story, even in those countries that have made significant progress, it is possible to point to failures. In the UK, for

Fig. 7.5 Selected pesticides in human adipose tissue in the United States, 1970–83.

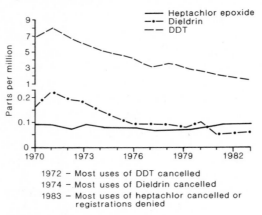

Parts per million

Heptachlor epoxide
Dieldrin
DDT

1972 – Most uses of DDT cancelled
1974 – Most uses of Dieldrin cancelled
1983 – Most uses of heptachlor cancelled or registrations denied

Source: US Environmental Protection Agency.

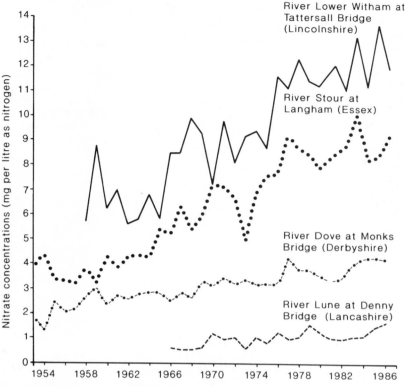

Fig. 7.6 River water quality: annual mean nitrate concentrations.

Source: Department of the Environment.

Note: All four rivers showed an upward trend in nitrate concentrations over the period. Concentrations have on average doubled over the twenty years; the largest increases tend to be found in areas with intensive arable farming. It is thought that changes in agricultural practices, including increased fertilizer use, were a major contributor to the rising trend.

example, there has been little overall improvement in river quality and the problem of nitrate pollution has been steadily increasing (Fig. 7.6); more generally, major challenges are presented by the 70,000 or so chemicals that were in use before the introduction of stringent testing, by increasing quantities of toxic and radioactive waste, by traffic pollution and congestion in cities, by carbon dioxide emissions and by continuing threats to species and habitats from development and resource exploitation. Large-scale problems of deforestation, erosion and desertification continue to threaten the environment of many developing countries. Although these issues are increasingly recognised and addressed by institutions and policy-makers all over the world, they are often extremely complex, have major economic repercussions and require international agreement for any effective action – all factors that contribute to notoriously slow progress towards legislation while degradation of the environment continues apace.

A recent comprehensive survey in the United States concluded that the country faced 'an array of environmental problems' more daunting than previous pollution crises, and that 'current policies and institutions, having addressed the easiest matters, seem increasingly unable to deal with these emerging problems'.[11] While there is not an immediate crisis, the Report argues:

> Looming ahead . . . is a set of complex, diffuse, long-term environmental problems portending immense consequences for the economic well-being and security of nations throughout the world, including our own.

New attitudes, new institutions and new policy instruments are needed if these more complex environmental problems are to be resolved.

Prospects

Optimists in the environmental debate of the late 20th century point to the evolution of public and corporate attitudes towards the environment, to the new political will for action at national and international levels and to the institutions and mechanisms already established which can translate that will into effective environmental policy. In the concept of 'sustainable development' (see Chapter 1), they see a means by which material wealth may be increased whilst at the same time the quality of the environment is enhanced and crucial environmental systems are protected. Environmental protection is seen as a positive process, which creates jobs and is entirely compatible with further growth of the economy.

More pessimistic observers see many problems with such a scenario. They point to the poor record of implementation of many existing environmental policies. They see major obstacles to progress in the lack of any global authority to expedite the process of international agreement and in the apparent insolubility of some of the worst potential problems (such as carbon dioxide pollution and global warming) within the existing social and economic framework. Most significantly, perhaps, some environmentalists reject the concept of green growth, arguing that a major re-orientation of values, lifestyles and expectations must be accepted if long-term environmental sustainability is to be achieved. As Jonathan Porritt, Director of Friends of the Earth, puts it:

> . . . sooner or later the realization will dawn on more and more people that solving the planet's problems is going to require breathtakingly radical action and international co-operation on a scale not seen since the Second World War.[12]

Yet even the more radical 'greens' acknowledge that there is considerable reluctance to start questioning the basic assumptions underlying our economy and society. Perhaps what divides them most sharply from those putting their faith in green growth is the question of time-scale. 'Sustainable development', by definition, involves limits, but the greener the growth, the longer it will be before such limits are reached. In the energy field, for example, there is undoubtedly much to be achieved through pollution control, clean technology and energy conservation. But technical, economic and aesthetic limits must ultimately imply a 'ceiling' beyond which further increases in energy supply and use become unsustainable. Similarly, although pollution from vehicle emissions can be very considerably reduced, uncontrolled growth in the number of vehicles on the road could soon cancel out these achievements – as well as adding to congestion and the demand for new roads, with their own set of environmental impacts. The fundamental policy questions raised by such considerations do indeed call for some reappraisal of taken-for-granted values and lifestyles. An important question is whether green growth gives us a breathing space in which to do this, or lulls us into a false sense of security that will make the ultimate transition more painful.

For the immediate future, however, the most urgent challenge must be to find ways in which to provide a good quality of life for all of the world's inhabitants without destroying the environmental systems on which we ultimately depend. Inevitably, this means further economic development, especially for the poorer countries, though we may find different and better ways in which to define and measure 'economic growth'. In all countries, there must be a new emphasis on the *quality of life*, involving economic, environmental and social dimensions. Prerequisites for environmentally sensitive development will be the genuine integration of environmental considerations into all policy areas, anticipation and prevention of further degradation and a spirit of international co-operation to tackle those problems that cannot be resolved at the national scale. Achieving these objectives presents perhaps the greatest challenge to the global community in the late 20th century.

Notes, references and further reading

Chapter 1

1   **Ward, B.** (1982) Foreword in **Eckholm, E.P.** *Down to Earth*, Pluto Press, London.
2   **Sandbach, F.** (1980) *Environment, Ideology and Policy*, Basil Blackwell, Oxford, p.30.
3   **Meadows, D.H., Meadows, D.L., Randers, J.** and **Behrenv III, W.W.** (1972) *The Limits to Growth*, University Books, New York, p.23.
4   Malthus is famous for a series of essays on the 'Principle of Population', written between 1798 and 1823. His well-known 'iron law' states: 'Population, when unchecked, increases in geometric ratio. Subsistence only increases in arithmetic ratio.' He argued against the charity of the Poor Laws, on the grounds that this would simply encourage the 'lower classes' to have more children. His essays had considerable influence, though his arguments have subsequently been discredited.
5   **Cohen, Bernard L.** (1984) 'Note of dissent' in **Simon, J.** and **Kahn, H.** *The Resourceful Earth*, Basil Blackwell, Oxford, p.566.
6   **Ehrlich, P.R., Ehrlich, A.H.** and **Holdern, J.P.** (1977) *Ecoscience: Population, Resources, Environment*, 3rd edition, W.H. Freeman & Co., San Francisco, p.4.
7   **Mishan, E.J.** (1967) *The Costs of Economic Growth*, Penguin, Harmondsworth, p.219.
8   *Ecologist* 1972, Vol. 2, no. 1: 'Blueprint for Survival'. Quotes from pp.21 and 22.
9   *The Times* Editorial, 14th January 1972.
10 **Crosland, A.** (1971) *A Social Democratic Britain*, Fabian Tract 404, p.5.
11 **Pepper, D.** (1986) 'Radical environmentalism and the Labour Movement' in **Weston, J.** (ed.) *Red and Green: the New Politics of the Environment*, Pluto Press, London, p.125.
12 **International Union for the Conservation of Nature** (1980) *World Conservation Strategy*, IUCN, Gland, Switzerland.
13 **World Commission on Environment and Development** (1987) *Our Common Future,* 'The Brundtland Report', Oxford University Press, Oxford, quote from p.37.
14 **Commission of the European Communities**, Fourth Action Programme on the Environment. See *Official Journal of the European Communities*, No.C/70, paras 23.1 and 24.1.

Further reading

See especially notes (3) and (13) above, which make an interesting contrast and show how the environmental debate has evolved. See also **Rees, J.** (1985) *Natural Resources*, Methuen, London, for a comprehensive treatment of resource issues at the global scale.

Chapter 2

1   **Bellamy, D.** (1984) Foreword to **Wilson, D.** (ed.) *The Environmental Crisis*, Heinemann, London, p.xii.
2   **Pearce, D.W.** (1989) 'Sustainable futures: some economic issues' in **Bothin, D., Caswell, M., Estes, J.** and **Ovio A.** (eds) *Changing the Global Environment: Perspectives on Human Involvement,* Academic Press, San Diego and London, pp.309–25.
3   **Heal, G.** (1981) 'Economics and Resources' in **Butlin, J.A.** (ed.) *Economics and Resources Policy*, Longman, London, p.66.
4   **House of Commons Select Committee on the Environment** (1984) *Acid Rain*, Fourth Report, Session 1983–84, HMSO, London, Vol. 2, p.16.

Further reading

Ashby, E. (1978) *Reconciling Man with the Environment*, Oxford University Press, Oxford.
Sandbach, F. (1980) *Environment, Ideology and Policy*, Basil Blackwell, Oxford.

Chapter 3

1   **Pryde, P.** (1972) *Conservation in the Soviet Union*, Cambridge University Press, Cambridge.
2   **Pearce, D.W.** (1974) 'Economic and ecological approaches to the optimal level of pollution', *International Journal of Social Economics* **1**, 146–59.
3   The London Brick Company controversy is described in full in **Blowers, A.** (1984) *Something in the Air: Corporate Power and the Environment*, Harper & Row, London.
4   **Rees, J.** (1985) *Natural Resources*, Methuen, London. Quote is from p.121.
5   **Brobst, D.A.** (1979) 'Fundamental concepts for the analysis of resource availability' in **Kerry Smith, V.** (ed.) *Scarcity and Growth Reconsidered*, Johns Hopkins University Press, Baltimore. Quote is from p.115.
6   For discussion of reserves estimates, see **Odell, P.R.** (1979) *Oil and World Power,* Penguin, Harmondsworth, and **Wildavsky, A.** and **Tenebaum, E.** (1981) *The Politics of Mistrust: Estimating American Oil and Gas Resources*, Sage, London and Beverly Hills.
7   **Heal, G.** (1981) Economics and Resources' in **Butlin, J.A.** (ed.) *Economics and Resources Policy*, Longman, London, p.72.
8   **Hardin, G.** (1968) 'The tragedy of the commons', *Science* **162**, 1243–48.
9   **Hardin, G.** (1974) 'Living on a lifeboat', *Bioscience* **24**, 561–68.
10 **Galbraith, J.K.** (1958) *The Affluent Society*, Hamish Hamilton, London, p.91.
11 **World Commission on Environment and Development** (1987) *Our Common Future*, 'The Brundtland Report', Oxford University Press, Oxford. Quote is from p.44.

Further reading

Holdgate, M. (1979) *A Perspective of Environmental Pollution*, Cambridge University Press, Cambridge.
Mitchell, B. (1989) *Geography and Resource Analysis*, 2nd edition, Longman, London.
Rees, J. – see note (4) above, especially Chapters 7 and 9.
Sandbach, F. (1980) *Principles of Pollution Control*, Longman, London.

Chapter 4

1   pH is a measure of acidity or alkalinity, on a scale from 1 to 14, with 7 being neutral. Lower numbers represent greater acidity. The natural acidity of rain is around pH 5.5.
2   **House of Commons Select Committee on the Environment** (1984) *Acid Rain* Fourth Report, Session 1983–84, HMSO, London. Quotes from Vol. 1: 31, 36, 37, 50; Vol. 2: 37–38, 41, 68, 191.
3   Synergism refers to the combined effects of two or more pollutants when this is more damaging than the impact of the same pollutants acting individually.
4   **Environmental Resources Ltd** (1983) *Acid Rain: A Review of the Phenomenon in the EEC and Europe*, Graham and Trotman Ltd, London, quotes from pp.8, 80–81.
5   **Elsworth, S.** (1984) *Acid Rain*, Pluto Press, London, quote from p.20.
6   **House of Lords Select Committee on the European Communities (sub-committee G)** (1984) *Air Pollution*, HMSO, London.

Further reading

The book by **Elsworth** – note (5) above – is a useful general introduction.

Chapter 5

1 **House of Commons Select Committee on Energy** (1987) *The Coal Industry*, First Report, Session 1986–87, HMSO, London. Quotes from pp. xlii, li, lii, lviii, 15.
2 **Turner, L.** (1985) *Coal's Contribution to UK Self-sufficiency*, Gower, Aldershot, Hants, p.45.
3 **Fothergill, S.** (1985) 'Alternative Job Prospects', paper presented at a conference on *Economic Prospects for the Coalfields*, November, Town and Country Planning Association, Sheffield.
4 **Commission on Energy and the Environment** (1981) *Coal and the Environment*, HMSO, London.
5 Greenhouse gases, like carbon dioxide, let solar ultraviolet radiation through the atmosphere, but trap infrared radiation, so that it cannot escape into space. The 'greenhouse effect' refers to the global warming that may result from this imbalance.

Further reading

Much has been written about the British coal industry but not all of the up-to-date material is very accessible. For a general background, see **Manners, G.** (1981) *Coal in Britain: an Uncertain Future*, Allen and Unwin, London.
For two very different views on pit closure, see:
Boyfield, K. (1985) *Put Pits into Profit*, Centre for Policy Studies, 8 Wilfred Street, London SW1E 6PL.
Glynn, A. (1985) *The Economic Case Against Pit Closures*, National Union of Mineworkers, Holly Street, Sheffield S1 2GT.

Chapter 6

1 A very interesting collection of 19th-century photographs was compiled by **Middleton, C.S.** (1978) *The Broadland Photographers*, Wensum Books, Norwich.
2 A more detailed discussion can be found in **Moss, B.** (1984) 'Mediaeval man-made lakes: Progeny and casualties of English social history, patients of twentieth century ecology', *Transactions of the Royal Society of South Africa* **45**, 115–28 and in **Moss, B.** (1987) 'The Broads', *Biologist* **34**, 7–13.
3 **Davies, G.C.** (1876) *The Swan and Her Crew*.
4 There is a longer account in **Lowe, P., Cox, G., MacEwen, M., O'Riordan, T.** and **Winter, M.** (1986) *Countryside Conflicts: The Politics of Farming, Forestry and Conservation*, Gower, Aldershot.
5 A Site of Special Scientific Interest (SSSI) is notified to a landowner by the Nature Conservancy Council and receives special protection from changes in use that would affect its conservation value.
6 The New Columbus Syndrome is a useful concept in environmental policy studies. It refers to the habit of those involved in policy- and decision-making processes either consciously or unconsciously to 'rediscover' problems long recognised by others – just as the fact that Columbus discovered America did not deter several others from laying claim to his unique triumph. The New Columbus Syndrome is a common tactical component in the non-decision-making process (discussed in Chapter 3).

Further reading

The book by **Lowe** *et al.* – see (4) above – is an excellent introduction to the wider issue of resource conservation and use conflicts.
Blunden, J. and **Curry, N.** (1988) *A Future for Our Countryside*, Basil Blackwell, Oxford.
The Broads Plan, produced by the **Broads Authority** (1987), contains a wealth of information and illustration on the problems of the Broads.

Chapter 7

1 **Lowe, P.** and **Goyder, J.** (1983) *Environmental Groups in Politics,* Allen and Unwin, London.
2 **Elkington, J.** and **Hailes, J.** (1988) *The Green Consumer Guide*, Victor Gollancz Ltd, London.
3 **Burke, T.** (1988) 'The business environment', in **Elkington, J., Burke, T.** and **Hailes, J.** (eds) *Green Pages: The Business of Saving the World*, Routledge, London, quotes from pp.20, 32.
4 Quoted in *Green Pages* – see note (3).
5 **Nickson, Sir David** (1988) 'Exporting environmental excellence', in *Green Pages*, pp.48–49 – see note (3).
6 **Wandesforde-Smith, G.** and **Kerbavaz, J.** (1988) 'The co-evolution of politics and policy: elections, entrepreneurship and EIA in the United States', in **Wathern, P.** (ed.) *Environmental Impact Assessment: Theory and Practice*, Unwin Hyman, London, p.162.
7 **Rees, J.** (1985) *Natural Resources*, Methuen, London, p.326.
8 **Carroll, J.E.** (1988) 'Conclusion', in **Carroll, J.E.** (ed.) *International Environmental Diplomacy*, Cambridge University Press, Cambridge, quotes from pp.276, 277.
9 **Worldwatch Institute**, Annual Reports, *State of the World*, 1776 Massachusetts Avenue, NW, Washington DC 20036, USA.
10 **World Resources Institute** and **International Institute for Environment and Development** Annual Reports, *World Resources*, 3 Endsleigh Street, London.
11 **Conservation Foundation** (1987) *State of the Environment: A View Towards the Nineties*, Washington DC, The Conservation Foundation, quotes from p.xxxix.
12 **Porritt, J.** and **Winner, D.** (1988) *The Coming of the Greens*, Fontana, London, p.263.

Further reading

A good summary of recent developments can be found in *Green Pages* – see note (3) above. The *State of the World* and *World Resources* Reports – notes (9) and (10) above – are also useful.
For a 'green' view of environmental politics, see **Porritt, J.** (1984) *Seeing Green: The Politics of Ecology Explained*, Blackwell, Oxford, and Porritt's subsequent book (note (12) above). It is an interesting exercise to compare this view with the manifestos of the major political parties.

Index